MORE

WORDS TO THE WISE

A Lighthearted Look at the English Language

To Carol —

Happy reading.

Michael J. Sheehan

MORE

WORDS TO THE WISE

A Lighthearted Look at the English Language

MICHAEL J. SHEEHAN

ARBUTUS PRESS
TRAVERSE CITY, MICHIGAN

More Words to the Wise: A Lighthearted Look at the English Language

Printed in the United States of America

www.Arbutuspress.com
Traverse City, Michigan

Library of Congress Cataloging-in-Publication Data

Sheehan, Michael, 1939-
 More words to the wise : a lighthearted look at the English language /
Michael J. Sheehan.
     p. cm.
 ISBN 978-1-933926-18-6
 1. English language--Usage. I. Words to the wise (Radio program) II.
Title.

 PE1460.S5174 2009
 428--dc22

                                  2008051598

DEDICATION:

To granddaughter Giavanna Haddock, who was at my side as I
edited this book, along with love to Gifford, Antoinette, Nikki and Lexi.

Also by Michael Sheehan

The Word Parts Dictionary, 2nd Edition (McFarland & Co., 2008) ISBN: 978-0-7864-3564-7

On the Lamb in a Doggy Dog World: At Play with the English Language (Arbutus Press, 2006) ISBN 978-0-9766104-9-6

Words to the Wise: A Lighthearted Look at the English Language (Arbutus Press, 2004) ISBN 0-9665316-8-X

The Word Parts Dictionary (McFarland & Co., 2000) ISBN: 0-7864-0819-7

Words! A Vocabulary Power Workbook (Harcourt Brace, 1996) ISBN: 0-15-502570-8

Handbook for Basic Writers (Prentice-Hall, 1991) ISBN: 0-13-381898-5 [co-author]

Workbook for Basic Writers (Prentice-Hall, 1991) ISBN: 0-13-381948-5 [co-author]

The Cry of the Jackal (Avalon Books, 1991) ISBN: 0-8034-8879-3

In the Shadow of the Bear (Avalon Books, 1990) ISBN: 0-8034-8838-6

PREFACE

Since the year 2001, WTCM-AM 580, a talk radio station in Traverse City, Michigan, has been carrying my radio program. Along with co-host Ron Jolly, I field questions each Tuesday morning about the English language. The topics include word and phrase origins, points of grammar and punctuation, pet peeves, pronunciation, funny gaffes in advertising and broadcasting, writing tips, and anything else remotely connected to our living, lissome language.

The questions contained in this volume were called in during the show or later emailed to me (wordmall@aol.com) during the past four years. They are real questions asked by real people, some of them confused by our mother tongue, some of them bemused by its jabs and dekes. As in the companion volumes written for Arbutus Press, the questions and answers have been edited for clarity and brevity, but the essence of the original interchanges has been preserved.

This is not a stuffy grammar book. Entertainment is on a par with instruction when you are in public media, but be assured that the answers are based on twenty-nine years of teaching experience, most of them at the community college level. If you love language, you will find questions in this book that *you* very well might have asked.

You'll find a thorough index to guide you where you might want to go, but the questions and answers are deliberately random -- just like the telephone calls that we field each week. As so many people have remarked when speaking of the first *Words to the Wise*, this is the perfect bathroom book: no chapters to confine you, and short questions and answers that can be read in any order whatsoever.

Finally, the program may now be heard in real time (Tuesday, 9:10 - 10:00 a.m. EST) in streaming audio. No matter where you are in the world, go to wtcmradio.com and click on *Listen Now*.

Michael J. Sheehan
verbmall.blogspot.com

MORE

Q. UESTIONS

AND

A. NSWERS

Q. I just had to share my pet peeve. I hate it when sports announcers say (as they so often do), "at the end of the day."

A. This cliché has gained currency. It's used just before giving the last item in a series, or it's used as a way to say "finally" or "bottom line." You're not the only one to hate it. *The South Africa Star* held a contest to find the most hated cliché, and this won. *Factiva*, a data mining company, found that American publications use it about 60 times a day.

Then there's the case of Lee Becks, a British teenager who really hates the phrase. He went to a tattoo parlor to have the Chinese characters for "love, honor, and obey" incised into his arm. To his chagrin, he later learned what it really said when he was picking up some Chinese take-out from a local restaurant: "At the end of the day, this is an ugly boy."

Q. What is the longest word in English?

A. Philosophically, trying to find the longest word in English is like trying to find the highest number. If a computer tried to generate the ultimate number, a little child could come along and say, "plus one."

Likewise, spell out the so-called longest word in English, and I can come along and slap on a *quasi-* or a *pseudo-* or a *non-*. That said, the longest legitimate word is probably the name of a chemical compound, but you'll never come across it unless you're a chemistry major. Pneumonoultramicroscopicsilicovolcanoconiosis, a miner's lung disease, is listed in the *Oxford English Dictionary*, but it calls it factitious. Floccinaucinihilipilification, pseudopseudohypoparathyroidism, and antidisestablishmentarianism are other candidates frequently cited.

It's all a quest for honorificabilitudinitatibus [*Love's Labour's Lost*, V.i.]

Q. My boy friend works part-time at a florist's making deliveries. He says that there's a hidden meaning in orchids, but he won't tell me what it is. Can you help?

A. Let's see. Lilac is for first love, ivy stands for fidelity, and the orchid symbolizes delicate beauty. Nothing hidden there. I think your boy friend might be referring to the etymology of the word. Orchid means testicles in a wide range of languages: Greek, Avestan, Old Irish, Armenian, Albanian, and Lithuanian. The image probably refers to

9

the flower's root, which has paired tubers. It gives new meaning to the slogan, "say it with flowers."

Q.   Are you ever surprised by what you discover about the English language?

A.   Indeed I am. It happened to me just recently as I looked up the seemingly innocent word partridge.

Partridges are members of the pheasant family. They eat insects, berries, and seeds, and they nest on the ground. Weighing less than a pound, they can run very quickly, which saves them from many a predator.

Then came a shocker: the name derived from a Greek verb, *perdesthai*, which, from antiquity, has meant "to fart." It's not so much that this particular bird is prone to flatulence. Rather, it refers to the noise made by the bird as it flies away. That has to be some takeoff.

Intrigued, I decided to do a wild card search on etymologies containing break wind, fart, and flatulence. That's when a second surprise erupted.

The German district of Westphalia was known for its pumpernickel, a coarse black bread not always fully appreciated. In fact, in early modern German, *pumper* meant fart. As the *Oxford English Dictionary* delicately puts it, "this type of bread was probably so called either on account of its being difficult to digest and causing flatulence, or in a more general allusion to its hardness and poor quality."

Hidden farts also lurk in lycoperdon (wolf's fart), a fungus puffball, Onopordon (donkey fart), a genus of thistles, pedicule (small fart), a louse, and poop, from a German verb meaning to fart.

Now I can't wait to have a partridge sandwich on pumpernickel. Pass the Beano®, please.

Q.   I have been meaning to ask you about something I heard Rush Limbaugh say a while ago. He used the expression "straw dog" in a way

---

QUICK QUIZ 1

Which one does not belong in this list?

(A) harangue (B) tirade (C) eulogy (D) diatribe

like "the straw that broke the camel's back." I have never heard of "straw dog" before. Where does that come from? Why do both meanings have a straw involved?

A.   That's straw in the farming sense—dry stems and stalks—not a straw as in drinking from a tall glass. The ancient Chinese used straw dogs in their sacrifices to the gods. They were carefully crafted to look real and fool the gods, but they were, of course, expendable. Fresh straw is a pliable material to work with, and when dry, it burns intensely. A famous quote by Lao-tzu (c. 604 – c. 531 B.C) mentions straw dogs: "Heaven and Earth are not humane. They regard all things as straw dogs...." [*The Book of 5,000 Characters*] Sam Peckinpah used the phrase as the title of his 1971 film.

The modern adaptation of this idea occurs in a business setting. There, a straw dog is a deliberately expendable idea floated in front of a client to make the *real* proposition look even better. Of course, it can backfire if the client has poor business sense and insists on using the mediocre plan. I don't know if this is how Limbaugh used it, but it's a standard enough metaphor.

"The straw that broke the camel's back" means the final minor irritation or burden that sends things over the brink. By itself, it would be insignificant, but added to all that came before it, it has serious consequences. It is related to the cliché, "that's the last straw," meaning that your patience is at an end.

Q.   In a recent show, you answered a question about the meaning of straw dog [*see above*]. I'm wondering about straw poll or straw vote. How does that fit in?

A.   A straw poll or vote is an unofficial poll or vote, taken to discover which way people are leaning or to discover hot-button issues. The results are not binding, but they may be useful to a pollster. The term is related to "throwing straws into the wind," a method used to this day by golfers to see which way the wind is blowing. As O. Henry once wrote, "A straw vote only shows which way the hot air blows." [*A Ruler of Men*]

Q.   Why do sportscasters call it a rhubarb when a scuffle breaks out on the baseball field?

11

A.   A rhubarb is a noisy argument that may lead to shoving. If it goes much beyond words, it can result in players from both dugouts spilling onto the field. *The New Dickson Baseball Dictionary* [Harcourt Brace, 1999] says that the word was popularized by radio sportscaster Red Barber. He said that he picked it up from a sports writer named Gary Schumacher, who credited another writer, Tom Meany, with its invention. So there's a clear trail, but why that particular plant?

The Oxford English Dictionary says that the word "rhubarb" was repeated by actors to give the impression of murmurous hubbub or conversation. It carried over from the stage to radio. *Radio Times* [Oct. 17, 1952] had this: "The unemployed actors had a wonderful time. We'd huddle together in a corner and repeat 'Rhubarb, rhubarb, rhubarb' or 'My fiddle, my fiddle, my fiddle' — and it sounded like a big scene from some mammoth production."

For some reason, I prefer "mudslide, mudslide, mudslide."

Q.   We live in an area rife with tourists. A walk along Front Street will take you past many stores selling T-shirts with slogans on them. My question is, is there a word for this touristy compulsion to buy and wear clothing emblazoned with place names?

A.   My personal favorite is, "If it's tourist season, why can't we shoot them?" but the Chamber of Commerce isn't amused. I'm not aware of any such word, but why not make one up?

My *Word Parts Dictionary* lists *-mania* as a compulsion or craving, *grapho-* as a term for marking or printing, and *hestho-* as a word part meaning clothing or dress. So get out there in conversation and in writing and promote the word hesthographomania: a touristy compulsion to buy and wear clothing emblazoned with place names.

Q.   Why do we call a stupid person a knucklehead? After all, a knuckle is a bone in the fingers, so joining it with head makes little sense.

ANSWER 1   (C) EULOGY

A eulogy is a speech filled with praise or positive comments.

Harangue, tirade, and diatribe are speeches filled with criticism or accusation.

A.   The word knuckle has evolved into that specific and restricted meaning, but originally a knuckle was the end of a bone at any joint, and it could be found in the knee, the elbow, and the vertebrae. It came from a Dutch word meaning little bone. So using knucklehead is the direct equivalent of calling someone a bonehead.

Knuckle plays a colorful role in many slang terms. A knuckle sandwich is a punch in the mouth. A pitcher may develop a knuckleball, a pitch using the knuckles in such a way that they impart an erratic spin to the ball. Getting near the knuckle is coming very close to a permitted limit. If you are up to the knuckles, your whole hand is in; you are committed to a project. If someone raps your knuckles, you have been reprimanded. A knuckle-duster is now called brass knuckles, and it's also a tight inside pitch in baseball. To knuckle down, from the game of marbles, now means to apply oneself earnestly. To knuckle under is to submit: picture a person kneeling on the ground, bowed over, leaning on his knuckles.

Q.   Is there a name for phrases that sound alike but are really different in meaning and spelling? I'm thinking of the childhood chant, "I scream for ice cream."

A.   You could call them homophones—words that sound the same but may have a different spelling, and certainly a different meaning. But for the type of phrase that you use as an example, one that confuses only when spoken, Gyles Brandreth [*The Joy of Lex*, 1980] used the term oronym. One of the meanings of the word part *oro*- is mouth, so I assume that's why he used that term. Other examples include *euthanasia vs. youth in Asia, some mothers vs. some others, peace talks vs. pea stalks, may cough vs. make off, Toyota vs. toy Yoda,* and *stuff he knows vs. stuffy nose.*

In his book *The Language Instinct*, Stephen Pinker wrote this: "[In speech] it is impossible to tell where one word ends and the next begins. The seamlessness of speech is... apparent in 'oronyms,' strings of sound that can be carved into words in two different ways."

If you'll excuse me, I have to submit an application for the Pullet Surprise.

Q.   Where did the phrase "to win hands down" come from? I heard a TV commentator use it in reference to a primary election.

A.   It means to win without much effort, and it goes back to the sport of horse racing. It's the counterpart of "keep a tight rein." A horse responds to subtle pulls on the reins, so a jockey will keep them tight to maintain absolute control.

But if he is very far ahead of the other horses as he nears the finish line, he can relax his grip and loosen his hold by turning his hands down. The *Oxford English Dictionary* gives this as an early use in print: "There were good horses in those days, as he can well recall, But Barker upon Elepoo, hands down, shot by them all." ['PIPS' Lyrics & Lays 155, 1867]

Q.   What is the context of Bill O'Reilly's "keep it pithy" remark? Does pithy come from "pit" meaning the core of the matter, as in a peach pit or olive pit? In other words, keep it short and to the central point.

A.   You have the meaning right—be brief, concise, and succinct—but not quite the origin. Pithy comes from the word pith, the soft internal tissue of a plant part. It also refers to the white and often bitter-tasting spongy lining under the rind of citrus fruits. So it tightly encapsulates the edible part in fruit, and it forms the no-frills core of other plants.

For the word pithy, the OED first cites Thomas More, 1529: "The sore pythye point wherwith he knitteth vp all hys heuy matter."

Q.   Why do they call a phony doctor a quack?

A.   It's used not just for someone who pretends to have a medical degree, but also for those who promote phony remedies, often making outrageous claims.

The word is a shortened version of quacksalver, a term that comes to us from the Dutch, where it meant a person who cures with home remedies. So at first, the idea of deception was not a feature. That slipped in around 1600.

QUICK QUIZ 2

Which one does not belong in this list?

(A) indigent (B) opulent (C) mendicant (D) impecunious

Quack in the original sense meant a scrap, kitchen leftovers. Salver brings to mind the word salve, as it should; it was an ointment.

Q. Is there a word for the practice of some celebrities to use only their first name? I'm thinking of Cher, Bono, Madonna, and the like.

A. Along with those, Beyoncé and Pelé use their first names, but Liberace used his last name. Maybe it's a generational thing.

A word with a different earlier meaning has been co-opted to cover this reality. The word is mononym, and in the 19th century, it meant a technical name consisting of one word only; dura and pia are medical examples. The *mono-* part comes from the Greek word for one, and *-nym* comes from the Greek word for name.

Q. Should I write, *"the mountains were <u>deceptively</u> near"* or *"the mountains were <u>deceivingly</u> near"*?

A. Go with deceptively. *Deceptively* refers to the possibility of a mistaken impression, probably not intentional. It's a matter of perception, right or wrong. *Deceivingly* suggests a conscious misrepresentation; something is deliberately misleading and fallacious.

So we'd write something like, "The castle on the mountain top was deceptively near. The guide deceivingly assured us that we would be there by dusk, even though he knew that the path ahead was blocked by a landslide."

Q. Why do we say, "I paid through the nose"?

A. This one is hard to trace. There's an explanation floating around on the internet that it's a reference to the Viking custom (ca. 9th century) of slitting the nose of any conquered person who didn't ante up tribute quickly enough. It made onlookers reach into their pocket faster. But this story has been discredited by careful researchers.

More likely, paying an exorbitant price is being compared to losing blood through a nosebleed—hence, the nose as the orifice involved. "Bleeding someone" has long been used as an underworld metaphor. We find the following in the 1666 *Leathermore's Advice Concerning Gaming*: "When [a gang of swindling gamesters] have you at the Tavern

15

and think you a sure Bubble, they will many times purposely lose some small summe to you the first time to engage you more freely to Bleed (as they call it) at the second meeting, to which they will be sure to invite you." [Eric Partridge, *A Dictionary of the Underworld*]

From the same year, the *Oxford English Dictionary* cites Giovanni Torriano's *Piazza Universale*: "Oft-times rich men engrossing commodities, will make one pay through the nose, whereas they might sell the cheaper."

Q.   Where do we get the phrase, "by and large"?

A.   It comes from the days of sailing ships. Originally, it meant "from all possible directions." Now, it means "in general; on the whole; everything considered; for the most part."

If the wind was blowing from behind a ship—from the stern—it was said to be sailing **large**. This was desirable, since sail adjustments would be held to a minimum.

If the ship was sailing into the wind (which it can do up to a certain point or degree), it was said to be sailing **by** the wind, signifying towards the wind.

Q.   Last night, my wife said at one point, "I think I'll have a snack; can I bring you something?" Whatever the reason, the word snack caught my attention. Where did it come from?

A.   Snack is a strange little word. We use it in contrast to a regular meal; it's just a morsel of food to tide us over. When it started life around 1400, it meant a snap or a bite from a dog. That evolved into a snappish comment, a jibe. By the late 1600s, it was a share or a portion of something, but not of food. It shifted its meaning to a wee sip of liquor, finally coming to rest in 1757 with our current meaning: "When once a man has got a snack of their trenchers, he too often retains a hankering after the honey-pot." [Monitor No. 90]

ANSWER 2   (B) OPULENT

Opulent means affluent, possessing great wealth.

Indigent, mendicant, and impecunious indicate poverty.

Now there are many compounds: snack food, snack bar, snack-sized, and so on.

Q.   Where did the theatrical term Box Office come from?

A.   Once again, you'll find many language legends on the internet claiming to explain this one definitively. For instance, there are attempts to take this one back to the Globe Theatre of Shakespeare's day. As people entered, we are told, they would drop the entrance fee into a locked box. If they wished to stand with the other groundlings, that's all it took. But if you wished to be seated, you walked over to the first tier of seats, where one more coin was dropped into a locked box. Finally, if you wished to sit in the upper tier with the gentry, one more coin was dropped into yet one more box.

I'm not sure whether that part is accurate or not, but the next part is where imagination was definitely inserted. When the play began, the story continues, all the locked boxes were taken to a room backstage, and the proceeds were counted. This room was known as the box office.

The problem with that part of the story is that the term doesn't show up in print until 200 years later, too long for it to have been lurking unnoticed since Shakespeare's day. From E. Sheridan, *Journal*: "After we had nearly reach'd the Box Office a cry of Pick-pocket raised a general confusion." At that point in history, a box office was the place where you could reserve a box (an enclosed area of seating) for that night's performance.

Q.   Is it true that the slang term for a police officer—cop—was formed because they had copper buttons on their uniforms?

A.   Another explanation is that it is an acronym for **C**onstable **O**n **P**atrol, but neither one seems to be correct. Instead, it is derived from the Latin word *capere*, to capture, lay hold of, or nab. That's one of their principal duties. The confusion about the buttons may be due to the extended form of cop—copper.

Q.   When I was in Florida last winter, I found this in a pamphlet from a Tampa, Florida, church: "Unbridaled lust causes one to sin." Isn't the first word spelled incorrectly?

17

A.   You bet it is; it should be unbridled. The image is formed from the idea of a horse and its bridle, the harness fitted around its head in order to control it. If a horse is unbridled, the control and guidance is gone, and it may become a runaway.

If there actually were a word spelled unbridaled, it would mean "having lost one's bride." Based on an internet search, the word seems to be in vogue as the name of a wedding fashion show and expo that features non-traditional wedding clothing and accessories.

Q.   My husband says that *normally* and *usually* are two words that are totally interchangeable. I say that there are differences. What do you say?

A.   One of the situations that I try to avoid is getting in the middle of a marital argument. As any police officer answering a domestic disturbance call will attest, that's a good way to get hurt. But this seems a bit more benign.

Unless I'm reading too much into it, I think that the two words have subtle differences. *Normally* means under normal conditions. That seems to put a slight emphasis on the external forum. *Usually* means done in a customary way. While a custom may apply to an entire community or just to one individual, it still involves personal choice: to conform or not. That seems to put the emphasis on the internal forum.

Q.   My grandfather had an odd saying that I never quite understood. He'd say, "She's moving like the tails of hell." The only thing I can think of is that the devil is often pictured with a tail.

A.   The confusion comes from the fact that he used an incomplete phrase. The original version was "the mill-tails of hell." A mill-tail is water that has passed through a mill wheel and is now moving rapidly downstream. So *the mill-tails of hell* was a way of expressing rapid movement, furious activity, or unstoppable force. Hell has often been described as a place of disorder and infinite apprehension. Here's an example from 1935, H. L. Davis in his *Honey in Horn*: "On a grade like this, you could drag the wheels and still be goin' like the milltails of hell."

Rudyard Kipling seems to have been the first writer to use the phrase *hell for leather*, which also meant extremely fast. (The leather reference was to a saddle.) When the phrase hit America, it became *hell-*

bent for leather. This would be speed with purpose and determination. And don't forget another phrase depicting rapid movement: *like a bat out of hell.*

Q. I have three children in the lower grades, and I have noticed that teachers are using the word *rubrics* a lot. It seems to mean a grading scale. What's your take?

A. It's what we called criteria or performance standards when I was teaching. It spells out what's important in a given task or skill; it lets the student know what must be included at each level to attain a specific grade. For example, a rubric for an essay might tell students that their work will be judged on purpose, organization, details, and voice.

The word rubric was originally an ecclesiastical term [< L. *ruber*, red]. The directions to the user of a missal, hymnal, or other liturgical book were written or printed in red ink. The priest, for example, would know that he was supposed to read aloud only what was printed in black ink.

Q. I was in the dentist chair today looking up at the posters on the ceiling, and I noticed one with a dog on it that said, "it's ruff being so doggone cute." Why do people say "doggone good"? I mean, it's really not a good thing when your dog is gone.

A. Doggone is another one of those minced oaths (like Jeepers Creepers), where people use a rhyming word or alliterative word to replace a sensitive sacred term. This one is a polite replacement for "Goddamn."

And it turns out to be a variation of the Scottish *dagone*, their way of saying "God damn." Other regional variations include dadburn, dagnab, dadblamed, and goldurn. So puppies have absolutely nothing to do with the word.

Some churchgoing people take offense even at these softened forms. As one Bible Church says on its website, "Remember, garbage is still garbage, even if it is placed in a nice container. We need to detest all curse words and realize that the substitutes stink as well."

Q. An e-mail that I received yesterday says that it was a common practice in the Middle Ages to stick a frog in a patient's mouth when he or she had a throat infection known as thrush. Hence the saying, "I have a frog in my throat." Is this true?

A. Give me a break! Just think about that alleged treatment: do you think that people would let some clown shove a frog down their throats when they could hardly breathe already? *A frog in my throat* is a colloquial phrase that refers to a temporary thickness in the voice, especially of a radio talk show host. It's an allusion to the hoarse, throaty croaking of frogs.

By the way, don't believe anything you read in that perennial email titled *"Life in the Middle Ages."* It is loaded with folk etymology—in other words, more imagination than truth.

Q. Looking around my neighborhood, I see an inconsistency in the names on the mailboxes. *The Smiths* are right across the street from *The Morgan's*. Should there be an apostrophe or not?

A. I believe that the plural form should be used—without the apostrophe. It gives the family name and signifies that X number of people with that name reside there.

Now, I know that some will say that the family name is being used in an adjectival sense with the accompanying noun merely understood: *The Morgan's (house).*

But that's still wrong. It would actually have to be spelled *The Morgans' (house).* First spell out the plural, then add the apostrophe; that's the rule. Even then, couldn't it equally be *The Morgans' (mailbox)*, *The Morgans' (property)*, *The Morgans' (driveway)*, or some other variation? It's simply too vague.

Of course, there's a very easy compromise. My mailbox simply reads *Sheehan.*

QUICK QUIZ 3

Which one does not belong in this list?

(A) adverse (B) inimical (C) antithetical (D) amicable

Q. Why do we use the expression "haul off," as in "I'm gonna haul off and smack you one" or "she hauled off and kissed me right on the lips"?

A. To haul off, according to the *Oxford English Dictionary*, is to withdraw or draw back a little before completing an action of any kind. Typically, there's a short-range backward motion followed by a forceful forward motion.

In the Dutch and Frisian dialects from which it developed, it meant to pull or to draw. It's considered slang in English, but many realism-oriented novelists found it a useful expression.

- Mark Twain: "Suppose he should take deliberate aim and haul off and fetch me with the butt-end of [a gun]?" (*Galaxy*, 1870)
- Damon Runyon: "Then Lily hauls off and gives me a big kiss right in the smush." (*Collier's* 20 Dec. 1930)
- P. G. Wodehouse: "I shall have no alternative but to haul off and bop him one." (*Jeeves in Offing*, 1960)

Q. Where does the phrase "my salad days" come from? I have an aging aunt who uses the term from time to time.

A. It's a roundabout way of saying "when I was young and inexperienced." There are many kinds of salads, but the traditional one has herbs and greens in it. In turn, green has been a synonym for young and immature fruits or plants since the year 1,000. From about the 14th century on, it was applied to untrained and inexperienced youth.

It seems that Shakespeare put the two together to create "salad days" in *Antony & Cleopatra*:

> My salad days,
> When I was green in judgment: cold in blood,
> To say as I said then!
> (Cleopatra in Act V, scene i)

Q. Why do people (including me) call Sault Ste. Marie "*The* Soo?" Does it go back to the French meaning of SSM and they're really saying "The Falls"?

A.   When people say, "the Soo," they are usually referring to the Soo Locks, not to the town name or to the falls.

But this ties in to a frequently-asked question, so I'm going to broaden the terms: when writing about geographical features, when do we use the definite article (the) and when do we leave it out? There are some guidelines, but there are plenty of exceptions and inconsistencies.

Don't use the definite article with the names of
- countries: China, Brazil, England. Exceptions: the United States, the Netherlands (groupings)
- cities, towns, or states: Detroit, Sault Ste. Marie, California.
- streets: Woodward Avenue, 42nd Street, Main Street.
- lakes and bays: Lake Michigan, Lake Victoria, Grand Traverse Bay. Exception: the Great Lakes (a grouping)
- mountains: Mount Everest, Mount Washington, Mount Rainier. Exceptions: the Alps, the Rocky Mountains (ranges or groupings)
- continents: Europe, Asia, North America
- islands: North Manitou Island, Easter Island, South Fox Island. Exception: the Aleutians, the Hebrides, the Hawaiian Islands (chains or groupings).

Do use the definite article with the names of
- rivers, oceans, and seas: the Amazon, the Atlantic Ocean, the Sargasso Sea
- canals and locks: the Erie Canal, the Soo Locks
- points on the globe: the Equator, the North Pole, the South Pole
- geographical areas: the Midwest, the Middle East, the Old West
- deserts and forests: the Gobi desert, the Amazon Rainforest
- gulfs and peninsulas: the Gulf of Mexico, the Sinai Peninsula.

ANSWER 3   (D) AMICABLE

Amicable means friendly, sociable, congenial.

Adverse, inimical, and antithetical signify antagonism or hostility.

Q. Why do some of your callers say that they're trying to stump the professor?

A. I believe that it's a figure of speech based on the difficulty caused by tree stumps when a farmer is trying to clear a field. "They happened to run their heads full butt against a new reading. Now this was a stumper." [Salmagundi (N.Y.) 20 March 1807]

Q. Which is correct—none of the cars was green, or none of the cars were green? I maintain that none is always singular because it means not one.

A. This one gets a little dicey, since none can also mean not any. An almost inflexible rule states that the verb number is ruled by one thing only—its subject. Any words coming between a subject and its verb are to be ignored as irrelevant.

However, there is a glaring exception when the subject is a quantity word, such as none, some, all, half, most, and so forth. In that case, you must factor in the words in the prepositional phrase—the of group. Here are some examples:

Some of the cheese **is** moldy.	Some of the hotdogs **are** moldy.
Half of the crowd **was** standing.	Half of the spectators **were** standing.
All of the ice **has** melted.	All of the cubes **have** melted.
None of the work **is** easy.	None of the jobs **are** easy.
Most of the crowd **was** stunned.	Most of the people **were** stunned.

The verbs in the left column are singular because the object of the preposition is singular. The verbs in the right column are plural because the object of the preposition is plural.

I repeat: this is an exception to the normal rule, where only the subject of the sentence determines verb choice.

23

Q.   One of my pet peeves is when people say aks instead of ask. Why do they do that?

A.   There could be a number of reasons: a misreading that is reflected in speech, a combination of letters difficult for that person to say, peer influence, the long reach of history, and so on.

Transposing letters is such a common process that it has a name: metathesis (from a Greek word meaning "to put in another place"). Whatever you do, don't confuse metathesis with metastasis, the spread of cancer cells.

Other examples are modren, brid, and the ever-popular nucular. But talk about a strange historical quirk: in old English, the verb to inquire was spelled *axian* or *acsian*, bird was spelled *bryd*, horse was *hros*, and wasp was *waeps*. In those cases, standard modern pronunciation amounts to transposed original letters.

Q.   In reading one of the O'Brian series, (viz., *The Fortune of War*, Patrick O'Brian, W.W. Norton & Co., NY, p. 138-139), I came upon the following dialog between Stephen Maturin (the ship's surgeon in the series) and Mr. Evans (the ship's surgeon aboard the USS Constitution)

Maturin: "...at breakfast this morning, Mr. Adams, who was also riz in Boston, stated that hominy grits cut no ice with him. I have been puzzling over his words ever since. . . ."

After barely a moment's pause, Mr. Evans said, "Ah, there now, you have an Indian expression. It is a variant upon the Iriquois katno aiss' vizmi - I am unmoved, unimpressed, yes, sir."

A.   The writer hastened to add that he knew full well that O'Brien was having a bit of fun with the reader—or, at least, the character Evans was having fun with the character Maturin.

The most likely origin was the practice of cutting ice blocks from a lake or pond to be used in refrigeration. Properly stored in an ice house with straw as insulation, these sizeable blocks could last well over a year. To cut no ice was to be useless to one's fellow workers. To be

---

QUICK QUIZ 4

Which one does not belong in this list?

(A) ratify   (B) abrogate   (C) rescind   (D) nullify

thorough, I should report that a few writers think that the phrase came from dull ice skate blades, which cut no ice and made traction harder. The heavyweights don't buy that.

Today, "cuts no ice" refers to an idea without influence or the power to impress.

Q. I'm curious about the phrase *can't hold a candle to* as in, "When it comes to cooking, Maria can't hold a candle to Charlene."

A. It means that a person or process is patently inferior to another: "When it comes to exciting sports, bowling can't hold a candle to ice hockey."

Commentators have noticed the inferior or menial aspect of it, and have come to believe that it refers to pre-electricity days when candles were king. An apprentice worker would hold a candle so that a journeyman could get the job done. If the apprentice couldn't even do that right, he was really at the bottom of the heap and didn't have much of a future in that profession.

This is the first written instance as reported by the *Oxford English Dictionary*: "Dise playars..that haue nothynge to playe for...Holde the candle to them that haue wherewyth, and wyll sette lustily to it." [Crowley, *Way to Wealth*, 131, 1550.]

Q. My burning question is the origin of the word "dibs," as in "dibs on the drumstick."

A. *Dibs!* is something that children shout out when they wish to lay claim to something. It might be food, as in your example, or it might be an object of some sort: "Dibs on the Lazy Boy when we watch the game!"

The *Oxford English Dictionary* tells us that it is an abbreviation of dibstones, a child's game in which one stone is thrown at another stone, perhaps a predecessor of the game of marbles (also known as mibs). Some say, however, that it was more like jacks.

John Locke used the original word in *Some Thoughts on Education* [1692]: "I have seen little Girls exercise whole Hours together and take abundance of Pains to be expert at Dibstones as they call it."

Q. What does the word **rub** mean in phrases such as *here's the rub, there's the rub, this is the rub,* etc.?

A. While rub has many meanings, the one relevant to your question started out as "an impediment or an obstacle that impedes the progress of the ball in the game of bowls." It didn't take long before it was being used in a figurative sense: "an obstacle, impediment, hindrance, or difficulty of a non-material nature."

It was in that sense that Shakespeare's Hamlet used it:

To be, or not to be: that is the question:
Whether 'tis nobler in the mind to suffer
The slings and arrows of outrageous fortune,
Or to take arms against a sea of troubles,
And by opposing end them? To die: to sleep;
No more; and by a sleep to say we end
The heart-ache and the thousand natural shocks
That flesh is heir to, 'tis a consummation
Devoutly to be wish'd. To die, to sleep;
To sleep: perchance to dream: **ay, there's the rub**;
For in that sleep of death what dreams may come
When we have shuffled off this mortal coil,
Must give us pause . . . .

Q. What is the asterisk *really* for?

A. What—is there a conspiracy or something? First, asterisk means "little star," a reference to its usual shape [*]. It serves a number of purposes:

- It can mark a footnote, especially if it's the only one on a page. In ads, some people call them fudge marks because they tend to take back what was promised.
- It can signify that a person is dead.
- Three spaced asterisks centered after a paragraph or section may indicate that the story will now leap forward in time.
- Asterisks might be used for emphasis, though italics are better. (And don't even *think* of using quotation marks for emphasis.)
- An asterisk may indicate that an ancient word form is a reconstruction or an educated guess.

- An asterisk may be used to mark a dubious word or statement.
- Asterisks may replace the middle letters in a vulgar or taboo word.
- Asterisks may indicate the expulsion of breath or some other body sound: *sigh*; *gulp*.

Q. Where did "spitting image" come from?

A. Originally, says the OED, it was *spit of,* then *spit and image.* "A daughter,...the very spit of the old captain" [Knapp & Baldwin, *Newgate Cal.* III. 497/2, 1825]

It deteriorated into *spitten image,* then somewhere along the way it was given the present participle form. In that form, it shows up in 1901: "He's jes' like his pa—the very spittin' image of him!" [**A.** H. Rice, *Mrs. Wiggs* vii. 94]

It means the exact counterpart or likeness of someone, often a parent. I've always thought that elements from the Bible resonate in the phrase.

- Genesis 1:27 "So God created man in his own image, in the image of God he created him..."
- Genesis 5:3 "And Adam lived an hundred and thirty years, and begat a son in his own likeness, and after his image; and called his name Seth."
- Genesis 9:6 "Whoso sheddeth man's blood, by man shall his blood be shed: for in the image of God made he man."
- John 9:6 "When he had thus spoken, he spat on the ground, and made clay of the spittle, and he anointed the eyes of the blind man with the clay."

Q. I have been trying to figure out something. Is there a difference between "done" and "finished"? I have heard people say they are "done" with something only to have someone else remark that "a turkey is done, you are finished." Is this correct?

A. I had an old aunt who used to say precisely the same thing. She was also the one who would say, "kids are goats; use the word children."

You will hear people who think that "done" is an inappropriate substitute for "finished," but they don't have a case.

The fact is, the word "done" has been used in the sense of "finished" since the 1400s. That's even older than my aunt. If someone is offended by that usage, you can always substitute the word "through": are you through with the paper yet? (*Through* is defined as "done or finished with" in the *American Heritage Dictionary*.)

Q.   Why are they called baseball bleachers?

A.   The root of "bleachers" is the verb "to bleach," which means "to lighten or whiten by exposure to the sun or by means of chemicals." When "bleacher" first appeared in English around 1550, it meant "one who bleaches." But by about 1889, Americans were using "bleachers" to mean "seating scaffold" or "grandstand."

If you expose colored cloth or a photograph to constant strong sunlight, it will begin to fade. The painted boards that formed seats on the bleachers would fade because they had no roof over them.

Q.   I was browsing through a computer magazine in my dentist's waiting room when I came across the word defenestrate. I wrote it down carefully so I could ship it on to you.

A.   You have the correct spelling. In Latin, *fenestra* means window, and the word defenestrate precedes computers by almost 400 years. It means to throw from a window, and one historical event in particular immortalized the word.

That event was the Defenestration of Prague. On the 21st of May, 1618, Bohemian insurgents broke up a meeting of imperial commissioners and deputies of states and threw two commissioners and their secretary

---

ANSWER 4   (A) RATIFY

To ratify is to approve and confirm.

To abrogate, rescind, and nullify is to disapprove and abolish.

out a castle window. Fortunately, they landed in a large pile of manure and survived. So to throw someone out a window was to defenestrate.

Flash forward to the computer age. Applied to computers, the term is a pun. In the mid 1990s, hackers used it to mean to exit a screen window. It also meant to strip Microsoft Windows from a computer and replace it with the Linux operating system. Bill Gates is not amused.

Q.   Why do we say "he's got bats in the belfry" to indicate that someone is crazy?

A.   First of all, in the modern sense, a belfry is the bell tower at the top of a church. Bats often congregate there, and at dusk you can see them stream out in pursuit of insects. Their fight is erratic as they dart hither and yon in pursuit of dinner. They know what they are doing, but to an onlooker, their flight patterns seem extremely disorganized—almost crazy.

Bats use echolocation to locate things and avoid obstacles, even in the dark. They emit ultrasonic sounds and use the reflection of that sound to chart their course. Thus, *blind as a bat* is a misnomer, since they don't depend on sight the way we do.

Bats and *batty* are also used to denote eccentricity or craziness. Fannie Farmer: "Are you bats," she said. [*Humoresque*, 1919] A. L. Kleeburg: "She...acted so queer...that he decided she was Batty" [*Slang Fables from Afar*, 1903].

Q.   My grandfather uses the phrase "smart as a whip" to mean highly intelligent. But a whip is an inanimate object; it has zero brains. Isn't it inappropriate?

A.   All I can say is that the phrase has stood for sharp intelligence and mental acuity since the 19th century. The Old English version of this word started life meaning sharp and stinging. A whip, when applied directly to horseflesh, stings and prompts quick reaction. In fact, when we receive an injury that gives a nipping, stinging sensation, we often say, "That smarts!"

Many commentators think that the brilliant cracking sound that a whip makes accounts for the idiom.

Q. Why do they call a military person "Troops"? I always thought a Troop was a group, not an individual.

A. I agree with you, but without an example in context, I can't begin to explain why someone used it. Troop comes from a Latin word that meant a flock. Originally, without the -*s*, the word meant a body of soldiers. By 1600, an -*s* had been added to designate the armed forces collectively, so troops is considered correct. But using troops for just one soldier has no justification.

Spelled as troupe (a band of players, singers, or dancers), the plural form survives without an -*s* ending. And when you're speaking of a Girl Scout Troop, the -*s* will not be there.

Q. I'm looking for an apartment, and the real estate agent who's helping me used the term "boilerplate lease." What is that?

A. Originally, a boiler plate was a steel plate used in making steam boilers. A number of identical steel plates would be bolted together, thus forming a very strong structure able to withstand the enormous pressure generated by steam.

In time, the term was transferred to a unit of writing that could be used repeatedly because it was durable and applicable to a number of cases. That's the sense in which it shows up in a lease. It also shows up in places such as the beginning of a DVD, where a standard FBI warning about duplicating the disk sternly appears.

In the old days (probably up to the 1950s), typesetters at newspapers used to set stories in lead lines that were bound in a framework plate which would be affixed to printing press rollers and inked. Paper from huge rolls would whip through the presses, thus producing the newspaper. Those plates were also called boilerplates.

Now boilerplate applies to computer coding that can be used repeatedly.

QUICK QUIZ 5

Which one does not belong in this list?

(A) adipose (B) corpulent (C) wizened (D) rotund

Q. Every school seems to have a mascot. What I'm wondering is, where does the word *mascot* come from? Say it often enough and it sounds weird.

A. It came into English from the French *mascotte*, meaning a charm, in the sense of a spell or enchantment. In turn, the French word ultimately came from a Latin word, *masca*, a witch. There was even an operetta by Edward Audran called *La Mascotte*.

So a cuddly mascot working the crowd into a frenzy and a witch share a common purpose: to achieve a goal by working their magic.

Q. I am wondering whatever happened to the word "disappeared." Did this word somehow "go missing" in the lost corners of life, only to be found there with the dust bunnies of time? What I despise the most is the current usage of the term "went missing" instead of the term "disappeared"; the media people who use such discrepancies "went missing" themselves.

A. This also annoys James Kilpatrick, among others. He refers to such constructions as "crabgrass idioms." I agree that it sounds funny to American ears, but you should know that in British English, no one pays any attention to this verb phrase.

It seems to be an amalgam of "went/is missing." The burden of the meaning is that someone went away, and now it turns out that this person is missing. It shows up as "gone missing," too: she has gone away, and now she is missing.

Even in American English, we deal routinely with *went crazy*, *went pale*, *went ballistic*, and the like. Probably the worst thing you can say about *went missing* or *gone missing* is that it is perilously close to affectation in American speech.

Q. Why is colonel pronounced like kernel?

A. The answer is history and its twists and turns. The word started life as the Italian word *colonelo*, the chief commander of a regiment. He led a "little column."

When it entered the French language, it became *coronel*. Both spellings, *colonel* and *coronel*, were assimilated into the English language, and for a while, both were accepted without a problem. In

31

literary use, however, colonel finally won out because it paid tribute to its Italian source.

Also, what started out as a three-syllable pronunciation changed in popular use to a two-syllable pronunciation: *col'nel* and *cor'nel*. By the time that colonel had taken root as the proper way to spell the word, people were already accustomed to the *cor'nel* pronunciation.

Q.   Is there much difference between envy and jealousy?

A.   What is this, a confessional? Actually, there are slight differences, enough so that the words are distinct.

Envy is a feeling generated by dwelling on the superior advantages or possessions of another. It can eat away at a person if not kept in check, but it's not always malevolent. Instead of wishing that the person would lose what he has, thus leaving it for me to grab, I might simply want to achieve the same level of success. Coexistence is possible.

Jealousy stems from the suspicion that there is a rival to my affections. There is a fear of being replaced by another person, leading to mistrust and apprehension. Both the loved one and the apparent interloper become the enemy. Coexistence is not possible.

Q.   Why do we say things like, "I love you to pieces"? What's so loving about breaking someone apart?

A.   You have a point. Many of the phrases that contain "to pieces" are rather negative: *broke to pieces, smashed to pieces, chew to pieces, tear you to pieces*, and the like. But for some reason, at the end of the 18th century it became a colloquial way to say completely, totally, through and through. Maybe it's equivalent to saying I love every little part of you.

Q.   Why is the letter –L- silent in words such as salmon and solder?

ANSWER 5   (C) WIZENED

Wizened means withered, dried up, shriveled.
Adipose, corpulent, and rotund refer to something
plump and full of juices.

A.   In those two cases, the spelling originally did not have an L. The fish was spelled samoun, and the fusible alloy was spelled soudur.

In the 18ᵗʰ century, our friends the hypercorrectionists decided that these and other words should show their Latin origins—*salmo* for the fish, and *solidus* for the joining agent.

Curiously, the silent L is often followed by one of four letters:
* D as in could, should, would, and solder;
* F as in calf and half;
*K as in balk, talk, walk;
* M as in calm, salmon, palm, and psalm.

Q.   I came across this word in a commercial. It is another word that appears to have changed its meaning through the ages. Should not WORTH-LESS mean that it is no longer valued at the original value? However, it now means "worth nothing."

A.   Oddly enough, the detached word LESS and the suffix -LESS are not the same word and do not come from the same word stem.

LESS as a detached word means "not as much as before," as you pointed out:

My account is worth less today than it was a year ago.

As my son matures, he blames me less for the loss of his goldfish. In Old English, *loes* meant small.

-LESS as a suffix means "not having; devoid of":

This cheap watch is worthless. [without value or worth]

I am blameless in this matter, your Honor.   [without blame or guilt] In Old English, *leas* meant free from or devoid.

This is a good reminder that some word forms that seem to be identical are mere spelling accidents.

Q.   People seem to love to use the word "penultimate" when describing something that is the very best. It's my understanding that it actually means next to the last or second best. Am I right?

A.   You are correct. They should be using the word ultimate to mean the best. Obviously, some people think that penultimate is some kind of intensifier.

This is one of the terms used to describe the position of the last 3 syllables in a word. This was important in classical Greek, where certain kinds of accents and pitches could or could not be used depending on the syllable.

The **ultima** was the very last syllable ("last"), the **penult** was one syllable back ("almost last"), and the **antepenult** was two back from the end ("before the almost last"). The adjectives for those words would be ultimate, penultimate, and antepenultimate.

Q.   Should it be handfuls or hands full?

A.   Actually, both are correct, depending on what you want to emphasize. Notice that the first one is a compound (single word) and the second consists of two words.

The general rule is that compounds ending in –*ful* (notice, just one L) form the plural by adding –*s* at the very end of the word. Thus, we have pocketfuls, shovelfuls, bottlefuls, armfuls, and so on. Avoid putting the –*s* in the middle of a compound: pocketsful, shovelsful, etc. That's increasingly being designated as wrong.

But when you use two separate words instead of a compound (bags full—two L's), the plural ending goes with the main word—the noun: pockets full of sand, shovels full of manure, bottles full of water, arms full of firewood, etc.

As for nuance of meaning, the compound (the one-word version) throws the focus on the item contained; the two-word version emphasizes the container itself.

• I had two hands full of peanuts, and that prevented me from picking up my beer.

• Grab a couple of handfuls of paper clips.

Q.   Why do we sometimes say, "me, myself, and I"? In other words, why the triple header?

QUICK QUIZ 6

Which one does not belong in this list?

(A) rancorous (B) benevolent (C) splenetic (D) malevolent

A.   Old English had equivalents for all three pronoun forms. Me was *mec*, myself was *me self*, and I was *ic*. When the phrase was cobbled together, I don't know. It's obviously meant to be jocular.

This is pure speculation on my part, but it is vaguely possible that "me, myself, and I" may have been influenced by Freud's tripartite view of self.

Freud divided personality into the id, the ego, and the superego. Only the ego is visible or on the surface. The id and the superego are hidden, but each has its own role to play in the personality.

The id represents instinct.

The ego is the surface of the personality, the part you show the world.

The superego consists of two parts, the conscience and the ego-ideal. The conscience censors and restrains the ego. The ego-ideal is an idealized view of one's self.

Q.   Isn't "Call a spade a spade" a racist proverb that should be avoided?

A.   Absolutely not. The spade in that proverb is a shovel, and there's an interesting story behind it.

The meaning is, use plain and blunt language. Say exactly what you mean; don't mince words.

When it was first devised in Greek by Plutarch, it read, "Call a boat a boat." That was later expanded (again, in Greek) by Lucian to read, "Call a fig a fig and a boat a boat." So why was boat changed to spade when the proverb came into English?

Erasmus was the perpetrator. The Greek word for boat was *skaphos* and the Greek word for digging with a spade was . . . *skaphos*! This happens in English, too. If I see the word *pool*, I need context to tell if it's a place for swimming or a game of billiards.

When Erasmus translated the proverb into English, he wrongly thought it was talking about a spade. So Erasmus ended up writing it this way: "I have learned to call wickedness by its own terms: a fig a fig, and a spade a spade."

I am well aware that spade has been used as a derogatory racist term, but that's <u>not</u> the case here.

Q.   I am perplexed about how the word media is used on national TV. When they say "the media ARE", I think they should say "the media IS". If I am correct, how can the media be so dumb? If I am the dumb one, please explain why.

A.   The natural tendency of English is to slap an -s- on the end of a word to signify a plural. So when we import a word from Latin or Greek—which have different systems to designate the plural—we run into confusion.

The singular form of this word is medium: *The medium of television is quite pervasive.* The plural form is media: *The media are drifting more and more under governmental influence.* But increasingly, the plural form mediums is being accepted as English conventions overcome foreign spelling rules.

So it's not a matter of being dumb. It's a case of foreign languages not always blending smoothly into English.

Q.   I'm sending you a couple of headlines from my local paper. Whoever writes them has a wicked sense of humor.

A.   Here's what my correspondent sent.
        • One headline read, "Analysts: finger food is not fatal." The lead sentence went on, "Sales have dropped sharply at Wendy's fast food restaurants in the area of northern California where a woman claimed she found part of a finger in a bowl of chili, but analysts say the company's long-term prognosis should not be affected." [Hmmmm.... digital technology in Silicon Valley.]
        • The sports section contained this gem: "Another school to test for 'roids." My first reaction was to picture some hapless school nurse clutching an industrial-sized tube of Preparation H, but the story merely referred to steroid use by athletes.
        [*Sheehan here again*] Later that week, in the same paper, an article in the sports section contained this sentence: "Andy still hunts, too,

---

ANSWER 6   (B) BENEVOLENT

Something benevolent is positive and promotes doing good.

Rancorous, splenetic, and malevolent promote ill-will and negativity.

from a wheelchair fitted with mountain-bike tires. He bagged the deer with a recurve bow that went into the ragu that evening."

Q.   Why does a dilemma have horns?

A.   OK—I'm guessing that you're referring to the phrase, "on the horns of a dilemma." If you're not, this answer will make no sense.
It means to be faced with two equally undesirable alternatives. It goes back to Greek philosophy, where a *lemma* was a premise in an argument, and a dilemma (two premises) was an either/or proposition.
The metaphor referred to a bull or ox with large horns, either of which could gore you.

Q.   I teach math at a junior high school, and I have just been offered the position of boys' basketball coach. I want to check something out. My college coaches used to holler at us to "suck it up," and it was useful advice that I'd like to pass on. But is this something I can say to youngsters?

A.   We all know that it's the equivalent of "be a man," and that it means to endure, to keep striving even in the face of pain, fatigue, or fear. It is heard most frequently on sports fields and in weight training rooms. I've even seen weightlifters wearing tee shirts with that slogan.
Chapman's American Slang, 2nd Edition, says that it was established by the 1980s and that it may relate to the military command, "Suck in that gut, soldier!" He gives no citation, however, which always makes me nervous.
I don't think there's even a slim chance that it refers to fellatio, if that's what you were worried about, but the word "suck" mentioned in an innocent context may titillate a group of pre-adolescent boys and cause them to snicker. (So will "titillate" for that matter!)
The bottom line is, by now, even the criticism voiced as "*that sucks!*" has been divorced from any sexual connotation. Listen to the kids; you'll hear them using it all the time.

Q.   There is an old saying among trial lawyers that goes something like this: "If you can't argue the facts, argue the law. If you can't argue the facts or the law, blow smoke."

A.   To blow smoke is a picturesque idiom. In the saying that you quote, it means to confuse, to set up a smoke screen. Picture a cigar smoker filling a room with clouds of smoke so that he almost disappears. It is principally an American term, but in the early 1800s, a British term for smoking was "blow a cloud."

A second meaning is to brag or to exaggerate.

Q.   The Federal Communications Commission made a ruling that the use of the F-word during the Golden Globe Awards program did not violate FCC policy. What on earth is going on?

A.   The pass was based on a technicality. Here is their own language: "The Federal Communications Commission defines indecent speech as language that, in context, depicts or describes sexual or excretory activities or organs in terms patently offensive as measured by contemporary community standards for the broadcast medium."

Their ruling said that while the F-word on commercial TV may be crude and offensive, in context it did not describe sexual or excretory activities. Rather, the performer used it as an adjective to emphasize an exclamation.

There's a wonderful window of opportunity here. Grammatically, the FCC says that using the F-word as a participle (a verbal adjective) is OK, but using it as a gerund (a verbal noun) is not. So I propose using the word "participle" as a polite substitution for the F-word. Thus, we'd be allowed to say, "Get your participle dog off my participle lawn, you participle moron."

Let's make this a national movement, folks.

Q.   When the new superintendent of schools was being considered for the job, our local newspaper said that the board "vetted" him. Is this something like being a veteran who survived a war?

A.   No. The word means to examine someone very carefully to see if he is fit for the position being considered. It started out meaning an examination of an animal by a veterinarian. Shortly thereafter, it was being used to describe a medical examination of humans. By the early 1900s, it had acquired its present meaning.

Q. In the phrase, "Cheezit, the cops!" where did the cheezit come from?

A. No one knows with certainty. "Cheese it!" or just "Cheese!" has been a cry of warning among criminals (and juvenile delinquents) since at least the early 19th century. The earliest citation for "cheese it" in the *Random House Historical Dictionary of American Slang* comes from an 1811 glossary that explains the phrase as meaning, "Be quiet; be silent; don't do it," the sort of thing thieves might whisper if they noticed that the cops were watching them. "Cheese it" has also come to mean "run away," especially upon sighting a police officer approaching.

The most popular theory is that "cheese" is simply a mutation of "cease," which would fit nicely with the "be quiet and act innocent" meaning of "cheese it."

Q. I wanted to share some history with you. The phrase "keep your nose to the grindstone" arose because it was important for millers not to burn the grain that they were grinding. If they kept their nose close to the millstone, they would smell smoke and know that they had to adjust the pressure.

A. I don't know how to tell you this, but that story is a fabrication. All the standard reference works say that the type of grindstone referred to in the proverb is the smith's one for putting an edge on a metal tool. The original form of the expression was "to hold one's nose to the grindstone" and the first example quoted in OED2, from John Frith's *A Mirrour to Know Theyself* of 1532 is:

This Text holdeth their noses so hard to the grindstone, that it clean disfigureth their faces.

This refers to sharpening tools with an emory wheel, not to the miller's trade. Subsequent citations confirm this. One example is from *Simple Cobbler*, 1647: "Salus Populi suffer'd its nose to be held to the Grindstone, till it was almost ground to the gristles, and yet grew never the sharper."

Q. When you write interrupted dialogue, you use ellipses to show that the words broke off at that point. "What on earth? . . ." My question is, what if the ellipsis is followed by identification words, such as, "he said." Do you need to add the usual comma?

A.   Old reliable, as I suspected, has the answer. In section 10:39 of *The Chicago Manual of Style*, 14th Edition, an entry titled FALTERING SPEECH [*you just have to love that heading*] has this example:

"But . . . but . . . ," said Tom.

The explanation reads, "Note also that in the last example a comma is used after the closing series of dots to separate the speech from the words identifying the speaker."

Then, on page 369: "If other punctuation, such as an exclamation point or a question mark, occurs at the end of the fragment, it is retained before the three points, as in, "The ship . . . oh my God! . . . it's sinking!" cried Henrietta.

Q.   All my life, I've had a great dislike of incense. It makes me sneeze and causes my eyes to water. Is there a term for such an aversion?

A.   Sure, any strong dislike or fear acquires a technical name if it is widespread. I was an altar boy in my misspent youth, so I breathed in huge quantities of incense smoke. My buddies and I used to compete to see who could disappear first in a thick cloud.

Anyway, there are a couple of terms: knissophobia or libanophobia.

Q.   Last night my church board members worked on some wording in the by-laws. There was a discussion of 'a historian' or 'an historian'. It was a question of whether it is an aspirate H. We know it's 'a history', but some felt historian was pronounced differently. Can you help?

A.   Pronunciation is sometimes a regional—even personal—affair. But in this case, the -h- is aspirated. Try lining up these words: history, historic, historical, historicity, historian, historiographer. In all cases, according to standard American pronunciation, the -h- is heard. So "a" is the proper article to use.

Interference can come from the other direction. If you believe in advance that *an* should be the article involved, when you say *an*, your

> ### Quick Quiz 7
>
> Which one does not belong in this list?
>
> (A) prolix (B) pleonastic (C) trenchant (D) garrulous

tongue will end up touching your top inner row of teeth. It is then much easier to simply move the tongue back and slide directly into the –i-sound: *an 'istorian*. But that is not the standard American pronunciation. The –h- sound must be heard.

Q. T-shirt: what does the T stand for?

A. It simply describes the shape of the garment when you open it out. The use of usually capital letters to describe shapes is fairly common. Aside from our T-shirt, we have A-frame, C-clamp, I-beam, O-ring, S-curve, U-turn, and V-neck.

Q. An absurd story, a hoax, is sometimes called a canard. Why?

A. It comes from the French word of the same spelling; it means duck, the water fowl. The *Oxford English Dictionary* says that it probably comes from a proverb: *vendre un canard à moitié* (to half-sell a duck). To half-sell a duck is much different than selling half a duck; it means not to sell it at all. So a canard is an attempt to sell us a tall tale.

An aircraft design that places the horizontal stabilizer ahead of the wing is also called a canard; picture the Wright Brothers' craft. It gets its name from the resemblance to a flying duck

Q. Why is gossip called scuttlebutt?

A. Originally it was "scuttled butt," a water cask (butt) set on a ship's deck with a hole in the top through which sailors could dip out drinking water. It was a cask with a hatch.

This is how Herman Melville put it in *White Jacket; or The World in a Man-of-War* of 1850: "There is no part of a frigate where you will see more going and coming of strangers, and overhear more greetings and gossipings of acquaintances, than in the immediate vicinity of the scuttle-butt, just forward of the main-hatchway, on the gun-deck."

If that doesn't sound like the equivalent of today's office water cooler, I don't know what does.

Q. I'm wondering about two things:

(1) I've heard people make such statements as, " I think I'll take a different tact," meaning a different course; shouldn't the word be tack? And does the word have a nautical derivation?

(2) What does the expression "by the board" mean, as in "that plan has gone by the board" (has become moot, or has been abandoned)?

A. As it turns out, both sayings are nautical in origin. Tack means to bring a vessel into the wind in order to change course. To facilitate this, a rope is attached to the corner of a sail, and it has been called the tack (something that attaches) since 1481.

All of this eventually led to the figurative sense of "a course or line of conduct or action." So, as you point out, "to take a different tact" is pure misuse—probably based on mishearing.

"To go by the board" is related to "man overboard!" The board is the side of the ship, and if you fall over the side of the ship you are swept away, gone forever. The figurative use of this phrase—a lost opportunity— goes back to 1855.

Q. Why is someone who is overly impulsive said "to shoot from the hip"?

A. "Shoot from the hip" goes back to the Old West. The secure way to shoot someone is to draw your weapon, extend it at arm's length (supporting the gripping hand with the other hand), check your sightline, and fire.

In a rushed situation, a cowboy would pull his weapon from the holster, get it hip high, then fire in the approximate direction of his target. It's a technique taught in self-defense classes to this day, but it works only if the bad guy is merely a few feet away.

Because shooting from the hip resulted in more misses than hits, the expression came to mean acting or speaking without sufficient forethought—hasty judgment.

ANSWER 7   (C) TRENCHANT

A trenchant argument is incisive, compact, and economical.

Prolix, pleonastic, and garrulous refer to wordiness and excessive length.

Q.   When we want people to be quiet, why do we say, "pipe down"?

A.   This is a reference to the boatswain's pipe, a small whistle used by the boatswain to give orders to the crew by playing a series of notes. A boatswain was the officer in charge of the deck; he was also called the bosun.

Every night, there came a time for the crew to stand down and go below. The leave the deck signal played by the bosun's pipe was meant to pipe the crew down below. The deck would fall into relative silence with the crew absent, so "pipe down" became the equivalent of "be quiet" or the cruder "shut up!".

Q.   What does *dollars to donuts* mean?

A.   It means a sure thing, and it usually appears in the form, "I'll bet you dollars to donuts." In other words, I'm so certain of my position that I will bet my valuable dollars against your practically worthless donuts. The OED tells us that it had some competitors: dollars to buttons and dollars to cobwebs. Alliteration won out. It also doesn't hurt that donuts have a hole in the middle that looks like a zero.

Q.   Where did "Holy Mackerel "come from?

A.   Like many such sayings (holy cow, holy smoke, jeepers creepers) *Holy Mackerel* is a euphemism for some sacred term that people don't want to utter. It's also called a minced oath. In this case, it's a euphemism for *Holy Mother of God*!

I like to find quirky uses of a term by using Google, and I discovered that Holy Mackerel is the name of a rock band, a seafood restaurant in Australia, a font family, and a cat treat.

The week after this question came in, I received a related one: "I had the bad habit of saying holy mackerel also. When we lived in France, I discovered that mackerel is some form of dirty word. I was so embarrassed; it did not cure me from saying it, but I did not say it in France!"

The answer came from my Francophile son: "*Maquereau* means mackerel, and it also is used to designate a cuckold, a husband whose wife has been unfaithful." (Cuckold comes from the cuckoo because it lays it eggs in other birds' nests and lets them hatch the eggs.)

Q. This headline came from the *Grand Traverse Herald*: "Attic art sale peaks interest." I'm pretty sure they meant *piques*—provokes or arouses. Agree?

A. You are correct. These days, peak (the noun) is a mountain top or the maximum point of development, achievement, or success. In its long history, it was a widow's hood, the pointed tip of a beak, the projecting part of cap, a pommel, lace with a scalloped edge, the narrow part of a ship's bow, a pointed implement, the highest point of a wave when surfing, and so many more.

Pique (the verb) means to stimulate curiosity. Earlier in its history, it meant to arouse anger. That came from a French word meaning to anger or annoy, so the meaning has evolved and softened over the years.

Q. Someone just asked me last night where the term "none of your bee's wax" comes from. Any idea?

A. I've seen two forms: "mind your own beeswax" and "none of your beeswax." Let me begin by listing where it definitely did **NOT** come from. An e-mail has been circulating for at least 5 years purporting to explain where common phrases came from. It is a joke, but most people take it seriously. This spurious e-mail says that years ago, when smallpox was rampant, women with the resulting facial pock marks would smooth out their looks by applying beeswax. When they were speaking to each other, if a woman began to stare at another woman's face she would be told, "mind your own bee's wax." This explanation is so silly that you'd think no one would be fooled, but it keeps coming back.

"Mind your own business" is a very old saying. Greek philosophers such as Plato used it, and you'll find it in I Thessalonians 4:11. (*Make it your aim to live a quiet life, to mind your own business, and to earn your own living, just as we told you before.*) Somewhere in the 1930s in America, either a childish mistake or a deliberate attempt at humor turned "business" into "beeswax." There is no connection to wax whatsoever. It simply says politely what would otherwise be a rather blunt and rude statement.

Q. You frequently see references to the majority whip or the minority whip. Why whip?

A.   This has an interesting origin. The word was originally whipper-in, and it referred to a huntsman's assistant who keeps the hounds from straying by driving them back with a whip into the pack formation.

It seems to have been William Makepeace Thackery, in his novel *Pendennis*, who used it to describe a member of Parliament whose job was to make sure that the members of his party showed up for voting and adhered to the party line.

Q.   I assume that the term "ticker tape parade" goes back to the old days in the financial district when information came on paper tape through machines that made a ticking noise as they printed.

A.   You're quite right that the original "ticker tape" parades, both in Chicago and New York, involved the use of paper tape from stock market machines that ticked as they produced buy/sell prices.

One of the summer jobs I had in high school was at the long-defunct *Chicago Daily News*. One of my duties involved running the paper tape from the machine through a handheld device (it looked like a flashlight) filled with water. The water activated the thin glue on the back of the paper, and a blade at the front end allowed you to cut the strips. What I was doing was setting up the stock market report for that evening's paper. I would paste the information on a ready-made form, one stock per line. The prompt for the cut was a stylized diamond; it signaled the end of the data for one stock and the beginning of another. When attention wandered from the boring task at hand—a relatively frequent happening— the financial section for that day would contain some illegible information. Good thing I had thick skin.

As to what they use now that everything has been transferred to computers, I have no idea. I've seen large bags of confetti and large bags of spiral-shaped paper tape at stores that cater to holidays, birthdays, weddings, etc. Perhaps that's what they use for those parades now.

The best part of it is that it allows the Streets and Sanitation Department to offer gainful employment to the brothers-in-law of ward politicians.

Q.   Dreadnaught is a type of battleship, but it's also a style of guitar. How did that come about?

A. That's right—the word does refer to a ship. Dreadnought literally means "fearing nothing," and it was the name of a ship in the Royal Navy around 1596 (Dreadenoughte). In the modern sense, it's the name of a class of British battleships launched in 1906. They had guns larger than anything seen before on a ship.

The Museum of Musical Instruments web site confirms that the guitar was named after the class of battleships. It was a large-bodied guitar with a full, resonant sound, something desirable for the driving rhythms of bluegrass, country, and folk music.

Q. We play a simplified version of skins in which you can win a hole with par or less if no one else cancels you out with a similar score. The question came up, where does the golf term "skins" come from?

A. This one is all over the landscape. A laughable explanation is that fur traders entering Scotland to do business, rather than look for a bath, a decent meal, or female companionship after months on the hunt, would opt for a round of golf, using the skins for betting. That one is so dumb that it needs no refutation.

Another explanation is that it derives from the idea of skinning an opponent, as in the statement, "he skinned me alive." There's an obvious reference to the fur trade again, but without the ludicrous aspects. As slang meaning to beat or overcome completely, it goes back to 1862.

A third line of reasoning comes from the United States Golf Association. "In other parts of the country, 'skins' is also known as 'cats,' 'scats,' 'skats,' or 'syndicates.' Of these, 'syndicates' seems to be the oldest term, going back at least to the 1950s, and possibly earlier. It has been suggested that 'skins,' 'scats,' etc., are simply shortened, simplified versions of the term 'syndicates.'" In turn, that meaning of syndicate probably derived from a 1934 application: "In Gambling, an association of people joined in a gambling or betting enterprise."

QUICK QUIZ 8

Which one does not belong in this list?

(A) exacerbate (B) disconcert (C) agitate (D) mollify

Finally, the *Oxford English Dictionary* tells us that skin started out as a name for a pocketbook or wallet, and in 1930 was already American slang for a dollar.

Or so a little birdie told me.

Q. "To peter out" means to run out gradually. Do you know where it came from?

A. There's no certainty on this one. One theory says that it was a mining term. Saltpeter (potassium nitrate) was used as a component of explosives. The miners called it peter, and they used it to blow up rock faces to expose veins of ore. When the vein ran out, it was said to have petered out.

Another theory is that it comes from the French *péter*, to fart, which appears in the English *petard*, a medieval military explosive device. Shakespeare made the word memorable in *Hamlet* with "hoist by his own petard." So, to peter out would be to fizzle out, as it were, under this explanation.

Q. My grandfather used to say "criminitely!" when something startled him. Why?

A. I don't know; maybe he was a high strung sort of person. Seriously, though, criminitely is another one of those minced oaths, a substitute for a word that a person regards as sacred, something not to be uttered outside of a prayerful situation. In this case, it's a substitute for the name Christ.

It's a variation on criminy, a word that the *Oxford English Dictionary* describes as "a vulgar exclamation of astonishment." It shows up in print in 1681, and the OED connects it to crikey and jiminy as attempts to avoid the appearance of profanity.

Q. When I was taking care of my niece the other day, I automatically used the words "upsy daisy" when I lifted her out of the car seat. It's a curious phrase, and we seem to use it only with children.

A. It's a common enough phrase, and the upsy part is self-evident. The OED suggests that the *–daisy* part is indebted to lackadaisy, an extended form of lackaday. It also shows up in lackadaisical. The problem

47

is that lackadaisy means "woe to the day," and lackadaisical is used for a person in a blue funk. How that connects to a playful saying used with a child is far from self-evident.

A similar-sounding phrase is "whoopsie-daisy," a variation on *whoops!*—an exclamation that we use when surprised or embarrassed. Adding the *–daisy* may simply have been a bleedover from the earlier form. A contemporary British colloquialism, to do whoopsies, means to defecate.

Q.   Could you comment on the saying, "take it with a grain of salt"?

A.   It means that you should be skeptical of what you have read or heard; it may not be completely accurate. As with so many old sayings, there is some disagreement about how it started.

Some say that it is based on the idea that food tastes better and is easier to swallow if you add a little salt. So just as something near its expiration date may be rescued by adding salt, so may a dubious statement become a bit more palatable.

Others say that Pliny referred to the custom of taking a grain of salt as an antidote against poisoning. Allegedly, it was found in the writings of King Mithridates after he was defeated in battle: "Take two dried walnuts, two figs, and twenty leaves of rue; pound them all together, with the addition of a grain of salt; if a person takes this mixture fasting, he will be proof against all poisons for that day."

A variation is to take with a pinch of salt.

Q.   What can you tell me about E-prime?

A.   It stands for English Prime, a modified form of our language. The chief modification is the total elimination of the verb "to be" [*be, am, is, are, was, were*].

ANSWER 8   (D) MOLLIFY

To mollify is to soothe and induce calmness.

Exacerbate, disconcert, and agitate stir things up and disturb.

Proponents dislike that verb for two reasons: they claim that it misrepresents certain realities, and that it leads to generalizations and fuzzy logic.

For instance, to say "Mike is a teacher" means that Mike = Teacher, as in A = B. In other words, there is total equivalence. It leaves out the realities that he is also a father, a son, a citizen, etc. My take is that if you're not rigid and overly literal, there's no way that an intelligent person would think that's all there is to Mike.

That the verb may misrepresent physical reality has some merit to it. If we say "the chair is red," we are violating the laws of optics. The chair actually isn't red. In white light, our rods and cones perceive it as the color we call red. And, of course, some colorblind people don't have a perception of red at all. Proponents of E-prime say that we should dump "is" and substitute something such as "the chair appears red to me." It is more precise, but I'd say that it depends more on one's knowledge of physics than of grammar.

I retired from teaching a few years ago, so I'm not in touch with how influential E-prime is these days. If it forces people to be accurate and logical, to avoid the passive voice, and to favor active verbs, that's great, but I was able to do that for years without jettisoning the verb to be.

Q.   Why do we say, "to get a leg up" to indicate that someone has an advantage?

A.   It is an equestrian term. When a rider in armor wanted to mount a horse but didn't have a box or block to act as a step, he would have to call on a helper. The rider would use his right leg to jump up, and the assistant would simultaneously boost his left leg up.

Q.   How did "no dice" come to mean *no way*?

A.   It may refer to the strength of evidence needed for a conviction on a gambling charge. *The Port Arthur [Texas] Daily News*, April 1921, describes a court case in which alleged gamblers were acquitted because the arresting officer admitted that he had not actually seen the dice. No dice meant that a conviction simply wasn't going to happen.

An alternative explanation is that in board games, when the dice land outside the playing area or do not end up lying flat, the turn is invalid: it is declared "no dice."

In any case, it means that something isn't going to happen—permission isn't going to be given. It shows up in Damon Runyan's *Guys and Dolls*, and it was a mainstay of hard-boiled detective novels.

Q. Is there a difference between initiate and instigate?

A. Initiate means to begin, to commence, or to start. It is a rather neutral, unloaded verb that simply points to the moment of origin. It comes from a Latin word that means to begin.

Instigate makes no pretense of being neutral; it is a loaded term. It means to cause something to start by stirring things up, provoking, goading. At its root is the idea of something being punctured by a sharp stick.

Q. When I send an email, I'm given the choice of sending a duplicate to myself, either with my screen name showing (cc), or with it not showing (bcc). What do the abbreviations stand for?

A. In the old days, when typewriters were state-of-the-art, copies were made by inserting a sheet of carbon paper between two regular sheets of typing paper. A copy in dark blue would appear on the second sheet. The letters cc at the end indicated that a carbon copy was being made, sort of a gentle warning to the recipient that other eyes would see it.

Even though some contend that cc in the age of computers stands for complimentary copy or courtesy copy, Microsoft Office Assistant still calls it a carbon copy, sort of an *homage* to the old days. The letters bcc, however, were not applied in the old days. They stand for blind carbon copy, something possible with computers, which contain layers of code.

Q. Why do we call it Indian summer?

QUICK QUIZ 9

Which one does not belong in this list?

(A) docile (B) refractory (C) restive (D) intractable

A.   Indian summer is a period of calm, dry, mild weather, with hazy atmosphere, occurring in the late autumn in the Northern United States. A Frenchman named St. John de Crevecoeur wrote a letter in 1778 that used the term:

"Sometimes the rain is followed by an interval of calm and warmth which is called the Indian Summer; its characteristics are a tranquil atmosphere and general smokiness. Up to this epoch the approaches of winter are doubtful; it arrives about the middle of November, although snows and brief freezes often occur long before that date."

There have been many attempts to explain why the word Indian is included. Some say that the region where the phenomenon was first observed was inhabited by Indians. Another explanation says that Indians called attention to it as the product of one of their gods. Yet another explanation is that this was the season that marked the end of their hunting season. As it happens, that's still the prime season for hunting deer.

Q.   Over the holidays my family divided into two camps:
(1) those who thought that nuts WITHOUT shells were called "shelled nuts" because they 'have been shelled' (like salted nuts 'have been salted'), and
(2) those who thought that nuts WITH shells were called "shelled nuts" because they 'have shells' (like salted nuts 'have salt'). What is going on here? Have we all gone completely nuts?

A.   Here's what a web site touting California walnuts has to say: "Clean and dried walnuts are stored until ready to be cracked by state of the art equipment to produce what are called "Shelled" walnuts, which also mean shell-removed." Nuts with the shells still on are called inshell nuts.

What's crazy is the language itself. Is a "criminal law professor" a law professor who has turned to crime, or a specialist in the field of criminal law? And a "small business owner"—is she the very short woman who owns the clothing store?

Once upon a time, when English was a youngster, these ambiguities didn't happen. The reason is that words that belonged together had endings that signified that connection clearly; our language was synthetic in form. Over the centuries, it evolved into an analytic language—position determines meaning (but not always clearly). If

51

"Darla loves Tommy," it's not the same as saying "Tommy loves Darla." Old Tommy boy may not even know that the girl down the street has a crush on him.

Latin is still a synthetic language. "Canis parva habet dominum magnum" can mean only one thing: "the small dog has a large owner." It doesn't matter where you move the Latin words. Because of its ending, parva (small) must be paired with canis (dog), and magnum (large) must be paired with dominum (owner).

But in English, everything depends on position: spelling doesn't change:

The small dog has a large owner.

The large dog has a small owner.

And "has the a owner dog large small" is unthinkable—and indecipherable.

Q. I frequently do crossword puzzles, and one word confuses me. The answer keys always spell the word for brown paper with a –K-, producing kraft. Why isn't that a –C-, as in paper used for crafts?

A. The word kraft is from the German word for "strong." It is a comparatively coarse paper noted for its strength, and it is made from unbleached pulp, with wood chips included. It's used in the manufacture of corrugated boxes, fiberboard tubes, shopping bags, etc.

Q. Where did "food for thought" come from?

A. It probably comes from a Latin phrase, *pabulum animi*, which some attribute to Cicero. [Actually, he used *pabulum ingenii*, food for the mind, in *Acad. Quaest.*, 4, 41].

Erasmus wrote, "Nor try to put courteous conversation into the minds of impudent men, for speech is the food of thought."

It shows up in a 1685 pamphlet titled *Coffee Houses Vindicated*: "Discourse is pabulum animi, cos ingenii; the mind's best diet, and the

---

ANSWER 9   (A) DOCILE

Docile means manageable and controllable.

Refractory, restive, and intractable mean obstinate and resistant.

52

great whetstone and incentive of ingenuity; by that we come to know men better than by their physiognomy."

In 1825 Robert Southey wrote, in *A Tale of Paraguay*: '"A lively tale, and fraught with food for thought.

Victor Hugo used it in 1865: "Animals are nothing but the portrayal of our virtues and vices made manifest to our eyes, the visible reflections of our souls. God displays them to us to give us food for thought."

Q. I heard the phrase "tilting at windmills". Can you explain its meaning?

A. "Tilting at windmills" goes back to Miguel Cervantes' 17th century classic, *Don Quixote*. The good Don (delusional, but decent-hearted) roamed the countryside, mistaking windmills for giants. "Tilting" refers to charging at an enemy on horseback, long lance extended. So, striving against something that isn't there, useless in advance, has led to applying this phrase.

Q. What is the plural of fish?

A. Both fish and fishes are used, with fish being fairly popular because it is usually viewed as a collective noun, much like deer/deer. But there are some interesting distinctions.

For instance, the Australian Fish Museum says that a group of fish of the same species are called fish—a school of fish. Two or more species of fish swimming together are called fishes.

Among other entities that use fishes with some frequency are the Florida Fish and Wildlife Conservation Commission, the Smithsonian Museum of Natural History, the California Academy of Sciences, and the University of Wisconsin.

My take is that icthyologists are more likely to use "fishes," and the general public is more likely to use "fish."

Q. Why do we foot the bill (pay up or settle) instead of elbow or knee the bill?

A.   Originally, to foot the bill was to add up all the charges and write the total at the bottom (foot) of the sheet. Eventually, that developed into actually paying the bill instead of just looking at the bottom line.

Q.   "To spruce up" is to make yourself neat and well groomed. I know that a spruce tree is fairly symmetrical. Is that the connection?

A.   There is no direct connection to the evergreen. Instead, spruce comes from Pruce, the Middle French word for Prussia. In the 15th and 16th century, Prussia exported many quality items: decorative coffers, fancy clothing, fine leather, and so on. To spruce oneself up was to dress in higher end garments from Prussia.

Q.   What is the difference between a colon and a semicolon?

A.   The colon (:) acts as a pointer within a sentence. It points to a list or an explanation that expands on what has just been said. *He loves two sports above all: soccer and rugby.* To replace a colon, use a dash. *He loves two sports above all — soccer and rugby.*
     The semicolon (;) joins two independent clauses that are closely connected in meaning. *A cause is a producer; an effect is a result.* Since an independent clause is a full sentence all by itself, you could replace a semicolon with a period. *A cause is a producer. An effect is a result.*

Q.   Where did the phrase "don't put your elbows on the table" come from?

A.   Some etiquette specialists claim that it originated in the Middle Ages when diners ate pressed so close together that if you put your elbows on the table, they'd probably end up in your neighbor's plate of food. Nowadays we have more room, but it's still regarded as an invasion

---

QUICK QUIZ 10

Which one does not belong in this list?

(A) prodigious   (B) colossal   (C) diminutive   (D) gargantuan

of personal space. And you increase the danger of knocking something over.

There's also the issue of hygiene. Placing extraneous items on an eating surface—items such as a briefcase, a purse, keys, elbows, or other body parts—is seen as spreading germs.

Q. Why is a statue showing only the upper portion of a person called a bust?

A. It's a bit difficult to find a definitive origin, but common sense would observe that the statue covers the portion of the body from the head to the breast (bust). It comes from similar French and Italian words that meant "the upper portion of the body," but not specifically the breast.

The *Oxford English Dictionary* also suggests that there may have been some influence cast by the Latin word *bustum*, a sepulchral monument that used an abbreviated human form as a commemoration of the deceased.

One of the most famous busts is immortalized in Rembrandt's 1653 painting, *Aristotle contemplating a bust of Homer.*

Q. When stocks go bad, they are said to be going south or heading south. Why?

A. Conventionally, compass directions are treated as up and down (north/south) and right and left (east/west). So when stocks decline, metaphorically they are going down, or south. In the background, there's also the image of a graph or chart, where highs are drawn up and lows are drawn down.

Q. I heard several people mention their pet peeves on your show last week, but I wasn't near a phone. Here's mine: everyone misuses the word *decimate*. If you check it out, it refers to the Roman Empire's practice of killing one-tenth of captured enemy troops as an object lesson. But now everyone uses it to mean a large number rather than its actual meaning.

A. Historically, you're correct. In fact, Roman commanders would execute one-tenth of any <u>Roman</u> unit that had the temerity to mutiny, not just foreigners. But you should remember that historical origins are not always frozen in place. Words can, and do, develop new meanings as the years roll by. And since 1663 (over 340 years ago) people have been using the word to mean, "to destroy or kill a large part of a group." You're not going to be able to turn back the hands of time.

Q.   Strike while the iron is hot. Where does that come from?

A.   It means to take advantage of favorable circumstances. It comes from the blacksmith's forge. If he didn't strike the metal with the hammer while the metal was flaming hot, he couldn't work the metal and beat it into the desired shape.

Q.   Why do we say that someone was hoodwinked?

A.   In the 9th century, "wink" meant to close the eyes completely, not the brief, flirtatious close/open motion that we mean today. The term was used to describe the practice of hooding hawks and falcons when they were carried. To hoodwink a person was to literally blindfold him with a hood, a covering made of soft or flexible material. This literal sense of hoodwinking was joined in the 17th century by the metaphorical sense of hoodwinking that we use today—to blind someone by trickery or deceit in order to take advantage of him or her.

Q.   What can you tell me about "walk the walk"?

A.   This is a figure of speech called ploce. It involves repeating the same word, but in a different sense. In this case, walk is first used as a verb, then a noun.
    The phrase probably arose in the African-American community, and it was a feature of a preaching style. In the 1950s, I used to listen to a Chicago R & B station that featured a DJ named Al Benson. One of his steady advertisers was Pekin Cleaners, and Al's tag line was, "You gotta

---

ANSWER 10   (C) DIMINUTIVE

Something diminutive is small.

Prodigious, colossal, and gargantuan refer to large things.

56

walk that walk and talk that talk and give it to me straight, 'cause if you ain't Pekinized, you ain't recognized."

An early instance of "talk the talk" is found in Mark Twain's *What Is Man? And Other Essays*: "I know several other trades and the argot that goes with them; and whenever a person tries to talk the talk peculiar to any of them without having learned it at its source I can trap him always before he gets far on his road."

Q.   Where does peanut gallery come from? My brother claims that it's a theatrical term, sort of like green room.

A.   It does have a theatrical origin. The peanut gallery was the topmost tier of seats in a theater, the cheapest in the house. For snacks, peanuts were sold; hence, the name. The worm had turned: in Shakespeare's day, the cheapest area was occupied by the groundlings, and the gentry sat up above.

If you're old enough to remember *The Howdy Doody Show*, a TV program from the 1950s, you'll remember that the young audience sat in bleachers named the Peanut Gallery. This was a pun, peanut being a colloquialism for a young child.

Q.   Why do they call one of the decks on a ship the poop deck? Is that where the sailors did their, er, business?

A.   The "poop" deck on a sailing ship is the aftermost deck at the ship's stern. It takes its name directly from the Latin word *puppis*, meaning "stern." Actually, the sailors did their business at the bow, where the wind would be behind them.

Poop also means up to date or inside information. It seems to be Army slang, and just before WWI, it was information that needed to be memorized. Poop sheet came to mean a bulletin containing the latest information.

Back in the 18th century, poop was a childish euphemism for defecation or for farting. It seems to have come from a 14th century use meaning "to make a short blast on a horn." I'm not making this stuff up. Check the *Oxford English Dictionary*.

Q.   Why do we say that something has gone haywire?

57

A.   Quite literally, haywire was the wire used to bind bundles of hay or straw. After it was clipped off the bales, the wire would often be used for makeshift repairs. Since the repairs were cobbled together, "hay wire outfit" became a contemptuous term for loggers using second-rate equipment (1905). A 1921 quote from *Outing* said, "You can't run a logging camp without snuff and hay wire."

It didn't take long for the term to be applied to shops, factories, and other businesses. Ultimately, the term was applied to people who are emotionally confused.

Q.   I'm trying to track down a word that my German father used. He called me hunyak. At the time I gave it no thought, but now I want to know if it was a term of endearment or a snide remark.

A.   I had a similar childhood experience, but in a different ethnic setting. My Irish parents called me *omadhaun* so often that I thought it was my middle name. Then I found out that it meant idiot.

I'm afraid that I have bad news for you. In several languages, hunyak is a disparaging term, though it can be applied in a humorous or teasing way. In Polish it means something like goof-off or clown. In Norwegian, it was close to bonehead. It probably started life as a contemptuous reference to Hungarians, then spread to other Central European locations.

Q.   The Three Stooges used to like the word nincompoop. Was that something they made up?

A.   No, it existed long before they appeared; it was already in use in the 17ᵗʰ century. Dr. Johnson tried to raise the bar by claiming that it came from *non compos mentis* (not of sound mind), but the OED doesn't buy that.

The "poop" part may have come from the derogatory term *poep*, a word that the Dutch applied to migrant German laborers. It meant clown or fool.

QUICK QUIZ 11

Which one does not belong in this list?

(A) equable   (B) roiled   (C) sedate   (D) irenic

The first half of the word poses some problems. It was originally spelled nicom-, and that has led to speculation that it was a reference to Nicodemus, a symbol for a neurotically timid person.

Historically, it referred to a Protestant living in a Catholic country in the 16th century who concealed his or her faith to escape persecution. Biblically, it is found in John 3:1. "Now there was a man of the Pharisees named Nicodemus, a member of the Jewish ruling council. He came to Jesus at night ..."

There have also been attempts to connect nincom- to ninny (simple because extremely innocent) and to noddy (a drooling fool who nods his head continuously).

Q. Why "souped up" hot rod? I know that some people have joined the fad of cooking food on their engine blocks, but that seems a stretch.

A. There are at least two opinions on this one. The first says that "soup" comes from supercharged and has nothing to do with the nourishing broth.

The second notes that the liquid took on many meanings: dense fog, the ocean, nitroglycerine, the foamy part of a wave, photographic developing fluid, and dope to enhance a race horse's performance. This theory posits a connection to the last item.

Q. A few military memoirs that I've seen in our local used book store contain the following as a title or subtitle: "I've seen the elephant." What's the connection?

A. To see the elephant, in a military sense, means to have engaged in combat. Before that, it was the equivalent of "been there, done that." It all started in small-town and rural America. The highlight of the season or of a young life was having the traveling circus come to town. One of the biggest draws was the elephant, an exotic beast compared to horses and cows. If you had seen the elephant, you had experienced all that there was to see. Later, as rural America migrated to large cities, it came to represent a loss of innocence.

Q. Why, when people are treated shabbily, do we say that they were shafted?

A. Shaft has many meanings, but the relevant one here is the narrow stem of an arrow or spear. In the old days of warfare, if you were shafted, not only were you wounded by the sharp blade, but the handle or shaft penetrated your body, too.

Q. What do you call the squiggly line that you draw on a check next to the dollar amount (in words)?

A. I checked the web sites of several banks and talked to a couple of bankers, and the consensus was that a <u>straight</u> line is added to prevent someone from changing the amount, not a squiggly one. But it may be a personal preference.

That said, leather workers have a word for the squiggly line that they often add for decorative purposes: a viner. There is also a mark used to indicate nasalization of a letter, such as the -n- in the Spanish *mañana*. It is called a tilde, and it was originally used in Latin to indicate an abbreviation. In math, x ~ y means that x is the equivalent of y.

Q. In the words boondoggle and boondocks, what is the **boon**?

A. I mentioned on air that boon was a Middle English word for a blessing or a benefit, but research reveals these two words have no connection to that meaning—or to each other, for that matter.

Boondoggle was a word invented by scoutmaster Robert H. Link to describe the braided leather cord worn as a decoration by Boy Scouts. It evolved into decorative leather gadgets, and ultimately, any wasteful project.

Boondocks comes from a Tagalog word meaning mountain; it was adopted by occupying American soldiers in the Philippines to mean "a remote and wild place."

ANSWER 11   (B) ROILED

To be roiled is to be agitated, disturbed, vexed.

Equable, sedate, and irenic point to a peaceful state.

Q. A narrow escape is often expressed by something like "I got away by the skin of my teeth." Where did that come from?

A. This colorful saying goes back to the *Book of Job*, 19:20 "My bone cleaveth to my skin and to my flesh, and I am escaped with the skin of my teeth."

Of course, any given tooth is not covered by skin. Teeth are embedded in the gums, but the outer coating is hard enamel. I think that the translator was using the word skin in the sense of "an outer coating or covering." Thus, we can speak of aluminum panels forming an airplane's skin.

Q. Why does" in a pickle" translate as "in trouble or in a difficult situation"?

A. We tend to think of pickle as the gherkin or cucumber that has been pickled, but originally, pickle was the briny, vinegary solution in which vegetables were soaked. The vegetables felt nothing, of course, but if you project how a human might feel if immersed in such a solution, you think of a stinging, burning, very unpleasant sensation.

Examples from John Heywood, Thomas Tusser, and John Foxe precede him, but Shakespeare uses it in the 1st act of the Tempest:

ALONSO: And Trinculo is reeling ripe: where should they
           Find this grand liquor that hath gilded 'em?
           How camest thou in this pickle?
TRINCULO: I have been in such a pickle since I saw you last that,
           I fear me, will never out of my bones:
           I shall not fear fly-blowing.

Q. When did the term elderly get redefined? On WGN news a couple nights ago, the death of a 61 year old female was discussed and she was called elderly. Even when I was a grasshopper, I never thought of the term in reference to anyone in their sixties or seventies. I am hunting for my Gray Panther costume as soon as I sign off.

A. In the old days, 65 (the official retirement cutoff) was considered the start of elderliness. These days, there is a case to be made that "elderly" is a synonym for frail; that means ignoring age and studying functionality.

Here's a compelling quote from the *Journal of Clinical Oncology*, April 1, 2005: "One should first ask the question: who is an elderly patient? While some regulatory authorities define elderly as a person older than 65 years, clinicians clearly understand that the definition of elderly is related to the pathophysiology of aging. The aging patients will present variable declines in organ function, and some, at age 75 years, will be as fit if not even more fit than many at age 60 years. This is the reason why geriatricians have taught us to objectively evaluate an elderly person, independent of age. Some geriatric physicians now define elderly patients as being more than 75 years."

In other words, define by stage, not by age.

Q.   Why is a street market referred to as a flea market?

A.   "Flea market" first appeared in English in 1922. It is a reference to Paris, where *Le Marché aux Puces* (literally, "market of the fleas") was a popular shopping venue. Flea Market got its name from the humorous suggestion that the piles of second-hand goods were infested with fleas. In fact, they may have been.

New York had a Fly Market which was situated in Maiden Lane on the East River side. It was a continuous operation in lower Manhattan from before the American Revolution until around 1816. The "Fly" came from the Dutch name for the market, "Vly" or "Vlie," which meant "valley," and was pronounced, "flea."

Q.   Why does "the whole ball of wax" mean everything?

A.   It may well be a humorous corruption of "the whole bailiwick." A bailiwick is a district or location under the jurisdiction of a bailiff, an officer of the king given administrative authority.

One of the early American uses referred to a real estate company and the location of its development, and a wick conjures up candle wax.

Q.   Where did "neck of the woods" come from?

A.   "Neck" had been used in English since the 16th century to describe a narrow strip of land because of its resemblance to the neck of an animal. (1540-1 R. Barlow, *Brief Summe Geographie* , 48: "Ageinst ramsey northest on the mayne londe is a hie nek of lande called sent davis heade.") Neck has also been used to describe the narrow part of a passage, a pass between hills and mountains, or a narrow channel or inlet of water.

Neck of the woods is a US phrase. While it existed in other forms in the early 17th century, it came into its own in that exact sequence in the early 19th century. (1839 *Spirit of Times* 15 June: "In this neck of the woods.")

Originally, it meant a narrow strip of wooded land. Gradually, the sense changed to refer to a region or neighborhood; trees were not a requirement.

Neck joined geographical feature names such as branch, creek, fork, hollow, gap, and flat. Noah Webster and other early Americans made it a matter of patriotism to come up with substitutes for British terms such as moor, estuary, heath, dell, and fen.

Q.   Why do some people say warsh (*warsh the dorg*) instead of wash?

A.   It shows up in a wide number of states, many of them a slash across the midsection of the country: Pennsylvania, Ohio, Indiana, Illinois, D.C., Oklahoma, Oregon, Iowa, Missouri, Maryland, Utah, Kentucky, and Nebraska.

It's common enough to have its own name—epenthesis, the insertion of an extra sound in a word. It shows up in Westminister, athuhlete, dorg, nucular, and after you warsh the clothes, wrench them in cold water.

Q.   When we have Summerfest in my home town, there is always a Carnival Midway. My question is, midway between what and what?

A.   When you walk down the central path lined by booths, exhibits, and rides, you are on the midway. In one sense, since you have tents and booths to your right and left, you are midway between the offerings.

But the real source of the name was the 1893 Columbian Exposition held on the south side of Chicago. The exhibits and rides were set up along the Midway Plaisance, a strip of land connecting Jackson Park and Washington Park. One of the many highlights found on the original Midway was the first ferris wheel, which stood 264 feet tall and carried 2,160 people at a time. When it stopped, you were midway between earth and sky.

Q. Why does baseball use the term battery?

A. In baseball jargon, battery was the word for "pitcher and catcher" considered as a unit. Henry Chadwick, 19th century sports writer and statistician, coined the term, drawing from the military sense of "artillery battery." This designated a number of pieces of artillery placed side by side for greater effect.

Deliberate or not, this also involves a play on words, since the pitcher and catcher are the only two players on the field that deal with the batter on every pitch.

Q. Why do some people say breakfastes for breakfasts?

A. As always, nonstandard pronunciation may be due to a number of reasons: mishearing, poor peer modeling, speech impediment, etc. Placing an extra letter at the end of a word—especially with the –sts– sequence—is not all that unusual. It makes it easier to pronounce the letters distinctly.

When a letter addition to the end of a word is done deliberately for historical reasons or to produce new forms, it is called paragoge. I suppose we could call this accidental paragoge.

I remember running into it in my teaching days. A student raised her hand during the first class of a new semester and innocently asked, "Mr. Sheehan, how many testes will we have in this class?"

QUICK QUIZ 12

Which one does not belong in this list?

(A) emote (B) ruminate (C) cogitate (D) ratiocinate

Q. It's my understanding that "green with envy" was coined by Shakespeare. True or false?

A. You're close. He used the phrase "green-eyed monster" in Othello (3:3), where Iago says: "O! beware, my lord, of jealousy; it is the green-eyed monster which doth mock the meat it feeds on." This is an allusion to cats, often green-eyed, who tease their prey before eating. In Merchant of Venice (3.ii.114) he uses *green-eyed jealousy*: "How all the other passions fleet to air, As doubtful thoughts, and rash-embraced despair, And shuddering fear, and green-eyed jealousy!"

Shakespeare described envy as the green sickness (Anthony and Cleopatra, 3:2). This may have derived from the condition that we would call chlorosis, an iron-deficiency anemia, frequently found in adolescent girls, that may give a greenish tint to the skin.

Ultimately, it all tracks back to the ancient Greeks and their theory of the four humors. Jealousy was controlled by an imbalance in bile, which they thought would cause your skin to take on a yellowish-green cast.

Q. When we like someone, we "cotton to" him. Why cotton?

A. Velcro would be better to express attachment, I suppose. Five hundred years ago, *to cotton* wool was to use friction to make it rise to a regular nap, particularly if you were joining different pieces of fabric. If it *cottoned well*, the result was satisfactory. It was a seamless joint.

By extension, it developed the meaning "to agree, to go well together." Finally, it signified "agreement with or strong liking for."

Q. An email revealed that "sleep tight" came from the old days when a mattress rested on a net of ropes. If the ropes sagged, you had a miserable time sleeping. You had to tighten the ropes, or sleep tight, to get a good night's sleep.

A. What did I tell you about emails explaining the English language and phrase origins? As soon as you receive one, hit the delete key.

The word *tight* in the phrase has nothing to do with securing sagging ropes. As an adverb, tight meant soundly or completely: Shut the door tight. I'm tight with him. It was a tight contest.

If you believe that email, then you must also believe that a *sound sleep* involves snoring.

Q. I have often wondered what the prefix "brand" means, as in 'brand" new car, "brand " new house, or Professor Sheehan's "brand" new book. It's like a song stuck in my head; why "brand"?

A. The original meaning of "brand" was "burning or fire," in this case specifically, a forge, kiln, or furnace. Something "brand new" was an item such as pottery or forged metal, fresh from the fires that formed it. The phrase dates back to the late 16th century. Shakespeare used the expression "fire new" to mean the same thing.

FABIAN: She did show favour to the youth in your sight only to exasperate you, to awake your dormouse valour, to put fire in your heart and brimstone in your liver. You should then have accosted her; and with some excellent jests, **fire-new from the mint**, you should have banged the youth into dumbness

Shakespeare: Twelfth Night, iii. 2. 16 – 27

A brand name is a trade name, and it is also connected with fire: to mark with, or as if with, a branding iron to proclaim ownership.

Q. Why do we say brown as a berry? I've seen a range of colors in berries, from red to green to black, but not brown.

A. Good question, and the answer may be rooted in the era in which the phrase originated. Let me first say, though, that I have purchased large, seedless grapes—sold as red grapes—that were actually a reddish brown.

Now, I say grapes instead of berries, because in Middle English, *berye* could also mean grape, even though the same word was applied to berries. And Middle English is the historical period that gave birth to the phrase.

ANSWER 12 (A) EMOTE

To emote is to act out based on feelings.

Ruminate, cogitate, and ratiocinate involve thought and deliberation.

It shows up in Chaucer's Canterbury Tales, specifically in *The Cook's Tale*. The original was "broun as a berye." Here's a translation.

> There lived a 'prentice, once, in our city,
> And of the craft of victuallers was he;
> Happy he was as goldfinch in the glade,
> Brown as a berry, short, and thickly made,
> With black hair that he combed right prettily

So there are a number of possibilities. One is that he may have been referring to a grape, and as I said, some grapes are reddish brown.

Another is that in Chaucer's day, the word *broun* was used for a very dark color, almost verging on black. So that would put blackberries and other dark berries into contention.

And finally, color perception is not universal. That is, things such as quality of light, time of day, the presence of bloom on fruit, its stage of growth, and a host of other considerations can alter the degree and intensity of what we see.

Q. Why do we refer to a fisherman as an angler?

A. An angle was another word for a hook, so a person who angles or fishes with a hook and line is an angler. It comes from the verb to angle, which has two meanings:

1. To use an angle; to fish with a hook and bait.

2. Figuratively, to use artful or wily means to get something that you want: to angle for a promotion.

There are two closely related phrases related to fishing and the use of a hook.

First, "fish or cut bait" is a saying that means make a decision; get on with what you're supposed to be doing or abandon the pretense. Contrary to what some think, this is not an admonition to cut your fishing line. Rather, it refers to bait preparation in which some junk fish is cut into strips to fit on the hook or to be used as chum. So the saying means, if you're not going to fish, at least help by preparing the bait for those who will.

The other phrase is "a can of worms." It refers to a complicated situation that should be avoided. Literally, it started out as a metal container with air holes and a handle that was used to carry worms to be used as bait. Open it up, and you have a squirming, wriggly mass of worms just itching to get out.

Q.   Why do some people say "a buck 3.80?" or "a dollar 2.94"

A.   I haven't found anything in print, so I'll have to hazard a guess. I'm convinced that "a buck" is their way of signifying the $ sign. It's like saying, "Dollar sign 3.80."
        If anyone has an alternative explanation, be sure to let me know.

Q.   How did we get the phrase, "sicker than a dog?"

A.   The earliest recorded use is 1705: VanBrugh, *Confederacy* II. i, "If..he shou'd chance to be fond, he'd make me as sick as a Dog." Common phrases in that same era were sick as a horse and sick as a cushion, of all things. Swift, *Polite Conv.*: "Poor Miss, she's sick as a Cushion, she wants nothing but stuffing."
        It's possible that it is a reflection of Proverbs 26:11. "As a dog returneth to its vomit, so a fool returneth to his folly."

Q.   Why do we speak of cutting a check? Wouldn't that make it valueless?

A.   That might be true if the phrase were "to cut up a check," but it's not. The answer goes back to the late 19th century, when, it seems, check forgery was a common event.
        Bank owners, especially in small communities where the margins of profit were tight, went to great lengths to prevent check tampering. When he issued a check, the owner actually cut numbers through the check so it could not be altered.
        The web site for Living History Farms, located in Urbandale, Iowa, shows photos of a check cutter.

QUICK QUIZ 13

Which one does not belong in this list?

(A) ephemeral   (B) evanescent   (C) transitory   (D) perennial

---

Go to http://www.lhf.org/cgi-bin/gygactivity.pl?320

Q.   I came across this strange saying in a *Farmers' Almanac*: "Since heck was a pup."

A.   Heck is an abbreviation of Hector, brother of Paris, the man who started the Trojan War by abducting the fair Helen. The story is told in Homer's *Iliad*, written about 1200 B.C. Pup means a young lad, so the saying means an <u>extremely</u> long time ago.

Since the 1600's, "to hector" has meant to harass and bully, which is rather odd, considering that Hector was a brave warrior who fought for his country's honor rather than for personal glory. In the 1920s, Hector was a very popular dog's name, so there's a hidden pun in *since hector was a pup*.

Q.   Can you find out the history behind the origin of the phrase, "Close, but no cigar"?

A.   Sideshow pitchmen at carnivals coined the phrase. The prize for ringing a bell by pounding a catapult with a sledgehammer was often a cigar. If you got close to ringing the bell but didn't actually hit it, you might be told "close, but no cigar." In other words, only perfection wins the prize.

Other games involving accuracy might also award a cigar as a prize. Ring toss comes to mind, as well as a shooting gallery with moving objects. These days, the prize is more likely to be a cheaply made teddy bear.

As a child, I remember that my buddies and I used to say, sarcastically, "Give that man a cigar." We'd use the phrase when someone did something that required no effort or said something that was painfully obvious. A cheap cigar had become a symbol of a worthless prize for an insignificant act.

Q.   Does "going to pot" stand for a man developing a pot belly—thus, being out of shape?

A.   That's an interesting image, but the phrase seems to refer to food in a different way. Around 1542, when the phrase first appeared, "to go to pot" was to be cut up like chunks of meat destined for the stew pot.

69

Such a stew was usually composed of leftovers, so "going to pot" was an appropriate metaphor for anything from a federal budget to an inquiring mind that had seen better days.

Q. Where did the saying "hair of the dog that bit you" come from?

A. It means that a small amount of what made you drunk might be used to cure a hangover. The saying appeared in John Heywood's *Proverbs*, published in 1546: "I pray thee let me and my fellow have a haire of the dog that bit us last night."

Much prior to applying it to a hangover, it was a folk remedy used to treat a dog bite. According to Pliny, the victim would place the burnt hair of a dog on the wound as a homeopathic remedy.

Q. To cut the mustard seems to mean "to pass a test" or "to meet a standard." How did it develop?

A. No one knows for sure where it came from. There are a couple of popular guesses.

(1) It is a corruption of "military muster," and therefore a perpetuated mistake. Muster was an inspection or roll call. To cut was to pass inspection. In a related use, if you're still on the team after the coach has eliminated the poorer players, you've "made the cut."

(2) When mustard is prepared it is cut—that is, blended—with vinegar to reduce the bitter taste. What we do know is that the word mustard was used as a compliment in the 1800s, probably because it added zest: *she's as keen as mustard; you have the proper mustard.*

Q. Why would I want to go to hell in a handbasket?

ANSWER 13   (D) PERENNIAL

Something perennial is enduring and lasts for a long time.

Ephemeral, evanescent, and transitory signify brevity and temporariness.

A. It's a case of personal preference. A handbasket is a light, convenient carrier for transporting things, so it indicates something easily and speedily done. An earlier phrase was *to go to heaven in a handbasket*, so we can see alliteration at work.

As early as 1629, it was *to go to heaven/hell in a wheelbarrow*. A bit later, *to go to hell in a handcart*.

Q. Where did scot free come from?

A. It seems to have had Scandinavian origins, and early on it was "scot and lot."

Scot was the total tax bill due, and lot was an individual's share of the total. It also applied to bar bills and to other types of tariffs. If you paid your scot, you met your financial responsibilities, Someone who went scot free got off without paying his or her share of the bill or tax.

Q. How did "spill the beans" get to mean "to divulge information?"

A. "Spill the beans" is first recorded in English in 1919; it means to accidentally disclose a secret. Let's look at both elements.

(1) The *Oxford English Dictionary* gives a 1574 quote for "spill it" meaning "to divulge, let out": "Although it be a shame to spill it, I will not leaue ['omit'] to say that which...his friends haue said vnto me."

(2) Beans has long been a slang term for information or knowledge, as in, "He doesn't know beans about baseball."

Over the years, there have been countless variations, all with spill. You can spill the works, spill the soup, spill what you know, and spill your guts.

WARNING: A phony internet story says that the phrase goes back to ancient Greece, where votes were taken by adding beans to a container: white for yes, black for no. If the judges clumsily knocked over the container, the judgment was prematurely revealed. The part about beans being used is true; the clumsy part is not. Remember, "to spill the beans" doesn't show up in English until 1919, too late for ancient Greece.

Q. Political commentators say that a candidate has thrown his hat in the ring, meaning that he has entered a race. Why a hat?

A.   Indeed, and why a ring? It means to enter a contest—now, usually political. In the early 19th century, it was a boxing term. To issue a challenge to an opponent, you would actually throw your hat into the ring. If the other person picked it up and threw it back, the fight was on. These days, when fewer men wear hats, the symbolism might be lost.

Theodore Roosevelt used it in the political sense in 1912 when he told a reporter, "My hat's in the ring. The fight is on, and I'm stripped to the buff." When former child star Shirley Temple announced her candidacy for Congress in 1967, *The New York Times* declared that she had thrown "her curls in the ring."

Q.   Have you noticed that news releases posted on the web favor made-up words?

A.   You were kind enough to include four examples, so here they are.
• Intrapeneur: Those who take hands-on responsibility for creating innovation of any kind **within** an organization. [< *intra*, inside]
• Entrepalooza: an annual seminar for entrepreneurs. [< lollapalooza, a remarkable or wonderful person or thing]
• Walktober: a fundraising walkathon held in October.
• Webinar: an online seminar conducted on the World Wide Web.

Q.   I read a lot about pirates, and I have come across the word filibuster, meaning a pirate. How does that connect to the political use of the word?

A.   This word started its life in the 16th century as a synonym for a freebooter—a pirate. It is probably a corruption of a Dutch word.

In the 19th century, the meaning was extended to cover one who engages in unauthorized and irregular warfare against foreign states.

Quick Quiz 14

Which one does not belong in this list?

(A) garrulous (B) taciturn (C) voluble (D) loquacious

By the 1880's, it finally carried the American meaning, "One who practices obstruction in a legislative assembly." Now we use it as the name of the action itself rather than a name for the perpetrator.

Q.   I know that a cataract is a waterfall, but how does that connect to the eye problem?

A.   In its original Greek form, cataract referred to the floodgates of heaven that held back downpours. When the gates were opened by the gods, people believed, it rained torrents. The word later referred to a waterfall, specifically one that fell straight down rather than cascaded over rocks.

The Greek word also meant a portcullis (a strong, heavy frame composed of crisscrossing vertical and horizontal bars used as a sliding barrier to a gateway) or grating on a window. It is from this meaning, not anything to do with water, that the figurative medical sense developed: "an opacity of the crystalline lens of the eye, or of the capsule of the lens, or of both, producing more or less impairment of sight, but never complete blindness." [OED]

Q.   Where did Jack O' Lantern come from?

A.   Originally jack-o'-lantern meant a man with a lantern; jack was the stereotypical British name for a male. The term was used to designate a night watchman.

In 1673, it was the local name for a will-o-the-wisp (technically, *ignis fatuus*), in southwestern England. The phenomenon involved phosphorescent lights seen at night on marshy ground. We know that it is the product of marsh gas, but in earlier centuries, superstitious people believed that they were sighting elves or fairies carrying flaming straw.

Later, it referred to turnips or pumpkins carved to look like a human face. By 1837, American English had embraced the "pumpkin with a light inside" meaning.

Q.   How about Tally Ho? Where did that come from?

A. It seems to be an altered form of the French taïaut, tayau, or tayaut, used in deer-hunting with hounds. The various French forms seem to be meaningless exclamations.

British hunters also yell Yoicks! or Hoicks! to spur hunting dogs on. Thanks to Sgt. Preston of the Yukon and other stereotypes, we have come to believe that Alaskan sledders yell "Mush, you Huskies!" to their dogs to urge them on. Mush comes from the French "marchez," the imperative form of "marcher," to advance, but it is not used as much as the command Hike!

Two terms familiar to horse handlers—Gee! and Haw!—are used to get the dogs to turn right or left. Another horse term (Whoa!) is used to get them to stop.

Q. When you go to a paint store, do you bring in a swatch or a swath of cloth to match the color?

A. A swatch is a sample strip cut from a piece of material. A swath is the width of a scythe stroke or a mowing machine blade.

There is also the archaic word swathe, to wrap in a bandage (as in the Christmas narrative's swaddling clothes)

Q. Should it be "$30,000 was set aside in savings" or "$30,000 were set aside in savings"?

A. For the most part, the rule that "a singular subject takes a singular verb, and a plural subject takes a plural verb" usually applies. One exception shows up in the question that you asked.

The heart of the exception is this: when you use nouns expressing time, distance, weight, money, and measure, they are singular if taken as a unit, but plural if referring to separate items. The $30,000 in your example is taken as a lump sum, not 30,000 individual pieces of paper money, so the statement should read, "$30,000 was set aside . . ."

ANSWER 14   (B) TACITURN

Taciturn means silent and untalkative.

Garrulous, voluble, and loquacious describe someone who can't shut up.

Here are other instances where an obviously plural subject is given a singular verb, thus forming an exception to the general rule:

- Ten minutes seems interminable when you are bored.
- Two blocks is not a long way to walk.
- Forty pounds is the standard weight limit for airline carry-on luggage
- Five dollars was required for the entry fee.
- In a wall, sixteen inches is the standard distance between the centers of adjacent studs.

The -s ending on these nouns proclaims a plural form, but the meaning is singular.

Q. I love the use of "slam" vocally to indicate an exclamation point. Is there a similar term for a question mark?" A friend told me to use the word *quirk*, but that doesn't sound right.

A. The *Oxford English Dictionary* defines quirk as a diamond-shaped piece of leather inserted at the junction of the fingers with the palm in some makes of gloves. It is also an irregular pane of glass.

But you might consider the word query, which means a mark of interrogation (?) used to indicate a doubt as to the correctness of the statement, phrase, letter, etc. to which it is appended or refers.
NOTE: You called the exclamation point a slam; other terms are also used:

- In typesetting or printing (and therefore when spelling text out orally), the exclamation mark is called a *screamer* or *bang*.
- Other slang terms include pling, smash, soldier, and control.

Q. Could you comment on these two sentences:
- Please **try and** avoid excessive noise in the lunchroom.
- Please **try to** avoid excessive noise in the lunchroom.

I was taught that the second version is correct.

A. Most grammarians will endorse your position, at least in formal writing or speechmaking. The tradition is that when the first verb is a command or a strong request (the imperative mood), the verb that follows should be in the infinitive form (to + verb):

Try **to avoid** excessive noise.

Come **[to] see** us when you get a chance.

Be sure **to get** an application form on the way out.

However, in informal use, the word *and* often replaces the word *to*:

Try **and avoid** excessive noise.

Come **and see** us when you get a chance.

Be sure **and get** an application form on the way out.

Remember that all grammar rules are arbitrary; they are not based on something inherent in the language, something that can never change. They are based on custom or style, realities that can and will change over long periods of time. Think of grammar rules as temporary conventions that may work for a few generations, sometimes longer. The only reason they are useful is to ensure that we are all on the same page. When the page turns and new rules evolve, there is no problem, no violation of something sacred, as long as we still understand each other. Understanding is the point; grammatical rules are merely a tool.

In practice, this means that the formal rule articulated above is not engraved in stone. Here's an example from 1813 that breaks the rule. The writer is Jane Austen, one of the finest English stylists in the last two hundred years.

"Now I will **try and** write of something else." [*Letter*, January 29, 1813]

Not even the Grammar Police will dare to arrest her for that.

Q.   Pipe Dream: is it a plumber's nightmare or a bagpipe-induced trance?

A.   I'm with you on those bagpipes. In this case, pipe dream has come to mean a goal that doesn't stand a chance of being achieved; it's totally unrealistic.

It originated with the opium pipe, a specialized pipe designed to vaporize opium (rather than burn it) as a delivery system. Its use became widespread in the 17th and 18th centuries in England, then spread to America. The point of smoking was to get high—to have a euphoric experience, a dream, as it were.

This is reflected in the literature of the time. Samuel Taylor Coleridge claimed to have been under the influence when he wrote *Kubla Khan*. Thomas De Quincy wrote an essay titled *Confessions of an*

English Opium Eater. Conan Doyle's Sherlock Holmes visits an opium den in one story, and Charles Dickens' unfinished novel, *The Mystery of Edwin Drood*, features the use of opium pipes.

Q. Should it be *surprised at* or *surprised by*?

A. Both are used, but some commentators maintain a slight difference.
•   *Merriam-Webster's Concise Dictionary of English Usage* promotes *surprised by* as the correct form to use when someone is taken totally unawares in a sudden attack: "The hunter was surprised by the charging grizzly bear."
•   When the emphasis is on "struck with wonder/excited to wonder," either one will do: "I am surprised at his boldness." "I am surprised by his boldness."

Q. My uncle used to refer to us as stinkpots. Now I wonder if it was an indirect reference to diapers, as in chamber pot.

A. "Stinker" applied to a young child often is a reference to diapers, but stinkpot has an entirely different origin.
The original stinkpot, a Dutch invention, was a type of hand grenade that gave off voluminous, suffocating smoke. It was used when forcefully boarding an enemy vessel in order to create a diversion. It was hard to fight back when you were choking and couldn't see.

Q. I'm stacking up wood for the winter, and I was musing: why is it called a cord of wood?

A. As you already know, a cord of wood is defined as a pile of wood eight feet long, four feet high, and four feet deep (though it can vary). It was named a cord because it was originally measured by a length of cord cut precisely. That way, you didn't have to worry about pesky inches on a ruler.
Cord, by the way, has an interesting origin. We think of it as string or rope, but originally it was animal gut.

Q. When I was a child, quarantine was way more common than it is now (chicken pox, scarlet fever, polio, etc.) Where did the word come from?

A. Quarantine, or a form like it, is common in Romance languages. Taken literally, it is a period of forty days, a number laden with symbolic freight. Currently meaning a period of isolation, the number of days can vary. It was applied to various situations:

- The Israelites wandered in the wilderness for forty years.
- Jesus fasted for forty days and nights before beginning his public ministry.
- Lent lasts for forty days.
- In the Middle Ages, some military service lasted for forty days.
- Newly-arrived travelers were placed in isolation to prevent the spread of infectious disease. Sailing vessels would fly a quarantine flag to signal to a host port that the ship was free of disease.
- Widows had the right to remain in a deceased husband's chief dwelling for forty days.
- Computers are isolated from the rest of the system (quarantined) when they are suspected of harboring a virus.

Q. Most political ads end with the candidate saying, "I'm Senator Smith, and I approve this message." Shouldn't that be "approve of"?

A. Not really. Approve means to officially sanction. That's what the candidates are doing, a legal requirement for political ads to promote accountability. To approve of means to think favorably of.

Q. Where did the word Pilgrim come from?

QUICK QUIZ 15

Which one does not belong in this list?

(A) acme (B) apex (C) nadir (D) zenith

A.   Americans will celebrate Thanksgiving soon, and the word Pilgrims will inevitably arise. Pilgrim is a word that was used by John Wayne in several of his westerns, usually addressing a stranger on his way through town. That was entirely appropriate.

The word started life in Latin as two words: *per* (through) and *ager* (field). This led to the word *pereger*, someone traveling abroad. That, in turn led to peregrinus, a foreigner. Over the course of centuries, this was transmuted in English to a form of pilgrim.

We have retained the fancy word peregrination to denote a journey, and we know that there is a peregrine falcon. In Gregorian chant, there was a Peregrine Tone, an unorthodox set of notes that wandered more than usual. And the British satirist Tobias Smollett wrote a novel titled, *The Adventures of Peregrine Pickle*, poking fun at the Grand Tour concept of his day.

Q.   I came across the word desuite in reference to a young lady. Any ideas?

A.   The only thing close that I could find is désuète (pronounced dayzwett more or less). If the reference was to her clothing, it means outdated, antiquated, and outmoded; thus, it was a putdown. If it referred to her manners, it meant old-fashioned and quaint, which could be construed as a compliment. Context is everything in this case.

Q. Where does the term "plumb bob" come from?

A. A plumb bob is a piece of metal suspended on a string. It is used to establish straight vertical lines. Often, the string is chalked and then snapped while taut to draw a perfect line.

The plumb part comes from the Latin *plumbum*, which meant the metal lead. It seems that the Romans used lead pipes to conduct water because the substance was easy to work with. Some have speculated that lead poisoning contributed to the downfall of the Roman Empire, but most authorities disagree. At any rate, the original plumbers were lead workers.

The origin of bob is uncertain. It may come from the verb *to bob* since the weight, when first dropped, bounces a bit. Fishermen are familiar with bobbers, plastic or cork floaters that bounce up and down with the waves, and mariners plumbed the depths by dropping a metal weight suspended on the end of a rope.

Another explanation points to the Middle English word *bobbe*, a cluster of fruit, due to a supposed resemblance between the chunk of metal and grapes. According to the *Oxford English Dictionary*, bob is still used in Scotland to designate a bouquet—or cluster—of flowers.

A versatile word, bob can also mean a knob, a sleigh runner, an earring, a knot of hair at the back of the head, a horse's tail docked short, a hair style, the weight on the tail of a kite, a lump of clay used by potters, and the grub of a beetle.

Finally, here's an early use of plumb line: "Thus He showed me: and behold the Lord stood upon a wall made by a plumb line, with a plumb line in His hand. And The Lord said unto me, 'Amos, what seest thou?' And I said, 'a plumb-line.' And said the Lord, 'Behold, I will set a plumb line in the midst of my people Israel: I will not again pass by them any more.'" [Amos 7:7-8]

Q.   Why do we say, right as rain?

A.   There have been expressions starting *right as* ... since medieval times, always in the sense of something being positive or satisfactory:

- right as a line,
- right as an adamant (a lodestone or magnet)
- right as a gun
- right as my leg
- right as a trivet
- right as a book
- right as nails

Right as rain is used in Max Beerbohm's book *Yet Again* of 1909: "He looked, as himself would undoubtedly have said, 'fit as a fiddle,' or 'right as rain.' His cheeks were rosy, his eyes sparkling."

No doubt the alliteration has helped it survive.

Answer 15   (C) nadir

A nadir is a low point.

Acme, apex, and zenith refer to high points.

Q. Last night's news had an item about a Manhattan penthouse going for millions and millions of dollars. Is penthouse somehow connected to pinnacle?

A. No. Penthouse started life as a simple lean-to with a single sloping roof. It turned into any annex, then was resurrected as a detached shed with a sloping roof. In the 1890s, it took on its present meaning: a flat, apartment, suite of rooms, etc., occupying the top floor or floors of a tall building. In Anglo-Norman, *pentiz* meant an outbuilding.

Q. I always thought the saying was "take the bad with the good," but I have been coming across its reversal: "take the good with the bad." Reversed, it doesn't make sense.

A. I hadn't noticed the reversal that was taking place until you wrote that you have been encountering, "you have to take the good with the bad." My sense is that the saying should be the opposite, as you believe, since accepting good things is so very easy and natural. We have to deliberately stir up a sense of proportion and balance to accept bad things; sometimes that takes significant discipline.

So I was surprised when I ran the Google test. 50,100 sites think it should be "take the bad with the good." 171,000 sites think it should be "take the good with the bad." I'm at a loss to explain why the reversal has taken place (there's no question that the original proverb put *bad* first and *good* last) and why it now enjoys a 3 to 1 margin.

It reminds me of the saying, "he's head over heels in love." Our head is *supposed* to be over our heels. It's topsy-turvy only if the heels are over the head! Research shows that the original 14th century phrase was "heels over head." Somehow, the order was reversed, and the one that makes less sense took over.

Q. What should we call the poles used when walking? How can ski-pole walking possibly make sense?

A. *Hiking poles* and *trekking poles* are the terms most often used by sporting goods sites. I've also seen *trail pole*. They differ from ski poles: some have adjustable sections for height, and some have internal springs to absorb shock. Cross country ski poles were adapted for this activity.

It relieves weight on the lower limbs. You use so much muscle mass that you match the benefits of walking in a much shorter time.

Q. I heard a commentator on CNBC make this statement: "His predictions go hat in hand with what other experts have been saying." Isn't that using the phrase incorrectly?

A. Yes. It should have been *hand in hand* to signify agreement and congruence. *Hat in hand* means to behave submissively. An inferior removed his hat in the presence of a superior as a mark of respect and obsequiousness.

Q. Does husky mean big and strong or does it mean fat?

A. It ranges all over the place, but tough and powerful predominate. Husky probably came from an Old English word that meant house. So at first, a husky person was strong and stout—not necessarily fat, but certainly not a stripling. (Reminds me of a phrase we used as delinquents: *built like a brick ****house.*)

In our day, it has become a euphemism for overweight. Walk into the clothing section of a store and you'll find husky sizes for boys and plus sizes or extended sizes for women.

Q. What's the difference between a boor and a bore?

A. Boor comes from an Old English word that meant farmer or husbandman, and that indicates the tenor of its meaning. It pointed to a peasant with a lack of refinement, a rude country bumpkin.

A bore is a tiresome person, a nuisance regardless of his social status. The origin is uncertain, but there is a slender chance that it is based on this analogy: a person who bores you is as annoying as a drill bit drilling its way into your skull.

QUICK QUIZ 16

Which one does not belong in this list?

(A) adamant (B) tractable (C) obdurate (D) pertinacious

Q. Where did the strange name Bluetooth come from?

A. It's strange only if you don't know history. The term came from Ericsson Mobile Communications, the company responsible for the technology intended to provide cable-free interaction among computers, printers, mobile phones, laptops, organizers, automotive devices, etc.

In searching for a symbol of seamless unification, someone recalled the 10th century Danish king Harald Blatand (Bluetooth in English). He united warring factions in Denmark, Norway, and Sweden in his day, so he was a great model of unification and collaboration.

Q. A story that has been told many times before is sometimes called a chestnut. That doesn't compute.

A. *The Oxford English Dictionary* confirms that it is a trite, predictable story, and though it labels it "origin unknown," it does point to the following incident.

Boston actor William Warren may have been the instigator of this term. He had played the part of Pablo in William Dillon's play, *The Broken Sword.* One of the characters in the play has the annoying habit of retelling the same old stories and jokes. Pablo interrupts him on one occasion as he begins the story of a cork tree with these words: "A Chestnut. I should know as well as you, having heard you tell the tale these twenty-seven times, and I'm sure it was a chestnut."

Warren was at a dinner party one evening when a fellow guest launched into a tedious story, and the actor whispered in a stage voice, "A chestnut. I have heard you tell the tale these twenty-seven times." The guests roared with laughter, and the story spread.

[See Brewer's *Dictionary of Phrase and Fable* and Linda and Roger Flavell's *The Dictionary of Idioms and their Origins*]

Q. I've heard *in the tank* used as what I believe means *to be beholden to.* Is that correct, and what is the source?

A. In the sense that you reported (*beholden to*), the phrase comes from boxing. To go in the tank is to deliberately lose a fight. That image was suggested by the phrase "to take a dive." There is secret collusion in the arrangement, so there is a pejorative slant.

Time Magazine: "The mainstream press was in the tank to Starr until the Starr report came out...." To be "in the tank to Starr" would mean that the press had not stood up to the special prosecutor as it should have. Here's another example from a Brooklyn blog: Is the Daily News in the tank when it comes to the Atlantic Yards Project? "The Daily News, owned by real estate mogul Mort Zuckerman, deserves scrutiny when it comes to the proposed $4 billion Atlantic Yards project, the largest ever in Brooklyn, to build a basketball arena plus at least 16 high-rise buildings. Let's acknowledge that the newspaper has the right to run numerous masthead editorials cheerleading for the Atlantic Yards project. Still, the rate of such editorials far outpaced any other daily."

In financial jargon, in the tank means performing very poorly. It is often used when prices for a sector or market are plummeting. The reference there is to a toilet tank; it's synonymous with "in the toilet" or "down the drain."

In sports jargon, it means that no energy is left, a reference to an empty gas tank in a car. *Rocky Mountain Sporting News*: "Foxworth left nothing in the tank. Cornerback cleared after hyperventilating in the locker room." [See *Southpaws & Sunday Punches and other Sporting Expressions* by Christine Ammer]

In police jargon, in the tank means in a common jail cell (drunk tank).

Q. Where did Quonset huts get their name?

A. In 1941, suspecting that global war was about to erupt, the United States Navy commissioned prefabricated buildings that could be shipped anywhere and assembled by untrained troops.

The George Fuller Construction Company was given the contract. They were located near Quonset Point, Rhode Island, and that accounts for the name.

Q. Have you heard the term snowclone?

ANSWER 16   (B) TRACTABLE

Tractable means easily managed and controlled.

Adamant, obdurate, and pertinacious mean stubborn.

A. Snowclone is a neologism used to describe a type of formula-based cliché which uses an old idiom in a new context. It was originally defined on LanguageLog as "a multi-use, customizable, instantly recognizable, time-worn, quoted or misquoted phrase or sentence that can be used in an entirely open array of different jokey variants by lazy journalists and writers."

- "If Eskimos have dozens of words for snow, Germans have as many for bureaucracy." [*Economist*]
- "Eskimos may have 18 words for snow, but Glaswegians have many more for getting drunk." [*Glasgow Leader*]
- That and **X** will buy you **Y**. Example: "That and a token will buy you a subway ride." Or "That and $3 will buy you a cup of coffee."
- There's a thin line between **X** and **Y**. Example: "There is a thin line between love and hate".
- **X** is the new **Y**: Pink is the new black. "Random is the New Order" [a marketing phrase for the iPod shuffle.]
- it's not the **X**, it's the **Y**
  "it's not the oil, it's the art"
  "it's not the price, it's the value"
  "it's not the carbs, it's the calories"
- "In space, no one can hear you scream" [ad for <u>Alien</u>] Google has 103,000 hits with the formula: No one can hear you…moan, pray, rock, say Doh, squeak, snore, sigh, disco, explode, yell fore.

Q. Why do we use the word "late" to signify that someone is dead?

A. Here's what the *Oxford English Dictionary* has to offer: "Of a person: That was alive not long ago, but is not now; recently deceased. *1490 CAXTON Eneydos vi. 28* Her swete and late amyable husbonde."

It seems that this sense developed from an adverb form that meant "not long ago, but not now." It then spilled over into the concept of death.

Q. This one's got me stumped:
If you or anyone you know IS interested, please call 555-1212.
or If you or anyone you know ARE interested, please call 555-1212.
To me, they both sound funny.

A.   Go with the first one, IS; here's the reason: When the conjunction **or** is used to join a compound subject (two pronouns in this case—*you* and *anyone*), the part closer to the verb determines the number of the verb. Since *anyone (you know)* is singular, the verb must be singular.

Here's a more extreme example using the negative *or*—the word *nor:*

Neither the teacher nor the students ARE here.

Neither the students nor the teacher IS here.

Both are correct because of the rule articulated above.

Q.   Has there ever been a time when the contraction of "am" and "not" has been used? I don't think I have ever heard amn't used and when you say it, it sure sounds funny. But is it grammatically incorrect?

A.   There have been various contractions for "am not," but they are still considered colloquial at best, illiterate at worst. I prefer the first school of thought.

One such contraction was an't. It shows up in William Congreve's play *Love for Love* [Act 3, Scene 7]: "I can hear you farther off, I an't deaf."

Then there is the dreaded ain't, which, among other meanings, can signify "am not." *The Columbia Guide to Standard American English* speculates that ain't might have developed from the form amn't, which would be much more difficult to say—hence, its mutation into ain't. But amn't is still used in some Scottish and Irish dialects.

The problem with ain't is its flexibility. It is used as a contraction for *am not, are not, is not, have not* and *has not.* It would be great if its meaning were confined to the first person singular (I am), but it is found in all three persons and in singular and plural situations.

The hope that H.L. Mencken expressed in *American Language* [1919] has not seen fruition: "Ain't is already tolerably respectable in the first person." Instead, we are now told to use the absolutely illogical wording "aren't I?" in questions—illogical because *are* is 2nd person

---

QUICK QUIZ 17

Which one does not belong in this list?

(A) alacrity (B) celerity (C) inertia (D) velocity

singular or all persons plural in the present indicative active. It is a glaring mismatch with I.

Q.   I had an aunt who used to chide us for lollygagging, and I've never been sure exactly what she meant.

A.   To lollygag is to dawdle, hang around uselessly, and waste time. That was the innocent side.

It also seems to have had a more licentious meaning. "Lolly" may have come from a Dutch word meaning to gag, and that slipped into northern English dialect as a word for tongue. So to lollygag may have been to French kiss.

Hendrickson's *Word & Phrase Origins* cites an 1868 edition of the Estherville, Ohio, *Northern Vindicator* complaining about ". . . the lascivious lollygagging lumps of licentiousness who disgrace the common decencies of life by their lovesick fawnings at our public dances."

Q.   Where did Holy Moly come from, and what does it mean?

A.   Moly was fabricated to rhyme with holy and it is probably a euphemism for Moses, Mary, or Mother of God. It joins *Holy Mackerel* and *Holy Smoke* as minced oaths. It was popularized by the Captain Marvel comic books.

Holy Moly is yet another example of a reduplicated rhyming compound. Other examples include killer-diller, helter-skelter, namby-pamby, legal eagle, and dilly dally.

Q.   What do you think of the word adverse in this newspaper story? "But company officials said the location of the gas station/convenience store remains 'a stumbling block' and that the company is **adverse** to making significant changes to its general store model."

A.   Along with you, I think it's a bad choice.
Adverse means antagonistic, harmful, unfavorable, opposing. Generally, it refers to things.

Adverse circumstances are tests of character.
Adverse criticism puts us on the defensive.

Averse means strongly disinclined, having a feeling of distaste for. Generally, it refers to persons.

The company is averse to making significant changes.

Many investors are averse to taking risks.

In this context, "the company is averse to making significant changes" is the better choice.

Q. I recall a taunt from my childhood. When someone acted in a cowardly way, we'd say he was yellow. We'd also say he was chicken, and chickens are yellow. Is that the connection?

A. Ultimately, it may have been connected to the Greek theory of bodily humors, which was revived in the Middle Ages. One of the components was yellow bile, an excess of which made one peevish, irascible, jealous, and cowardly.

The color yellow has had negative connotations for a long time. In France in the Middle Ages, the doors of traitors were smeared with yellow. In Spain, victims of the Inquisition were forced to wear yellow. At one point in history, ships with quarantined people on board had to fly a yellow flag. On the American frontier, a worthless person was a yellow dog. And Nazi Germany forced Jews to wear a yellow Star of David.

Q. Can you sort out 12:00 a.m. and 12:00 p.m.? In other words, which one means noon and which one means midnight?

A. On air, I gave an answer that I thought was eminently logical. If it's 11:59 p.m., then the next minute to tick by will take us into the wee hours of the morning, making midnight 12:00 a.m. One minute later, it's 12:01 a.m. Correlatively, if it's 11:59 a.m., 12:00 p.m. (noon) comes next, and a minute later, it will be 12:01 p.m. Piece of cake. Then I went home and did some research.

ANSWER 17   (C) INERTIA

Inertia in this sense implies lack of movement.

Alacrity, celerity, and velocity involve motion and speed.

It turns out that the *U.S. Government Printing Office Style Manual* puts it precisely the other way around. It says that 12:00 a.m. is noon, and that 12:00 p.m. is midnight.

Thoroughly confused, I sat down and did some thinking. It suddenly hit me that if you consider the nighttime 12:00 as the *first* minute of the morning, then it makes sense to think of it as a.m. However, if you think of it as the *last* minute of the evening, logically it's p.m. The same happens at midday: if 12:00 is the *start* of the afternoon, then it's p.m., but if it's the *last* minute of the morning, it's a.m.

So which viewpoint is correct? I have decided to heed the advice of the Greenwich Mean Time site. This summarizes their position: both a.m. and p.m. start at 12:00:01 if you are using a twelve-hour clock, not at 12:00:00. And both a.m. and p.m. end at 11:59:59, not at 12:00:00. If you were to write exact midnight and noon as transparent 6-digit numbers, they would come out as 00:00:00. In other words, they have no meaning; they are ciphers.

I compare it to the yellow stripe down the middle of the highway. That line is not part of the left lane, nor is it part of the right lane. It is the point of demarcation that divides right from left. Likewise, midnight and noon don't take sides; they are moments of demarcation.

So from now on, there's no 12:00 a.m. or 12:00 p.m. in my life; it will be noon or midnight. Better yet, perhaps I should switch to the 24-hour clock.

Q.   My husband and I listen to a local classical music station, and every day it offers a feature with an odd title. We'd like to look up the word, but we can't figure out how to spell it. It sounds something like uh-fum-uh-rus.

A.   One of the problems with our phonetic system is that the very same sound can be represented by more than one letter combination. Here you have a word that starts with the schwa sound (uh), which can be represented by any of the vowels, depending on the circumstances. It's followed in this case by the steady sound of air passing over the lower lip, held gently in place by the upper teeth. That could turn out to be f, ff, or ph.

The word you're looking for is spelled ephemeris, and it refers to an almanac or calendar that contains astrological or meteorological predictions for any given day: when the sun will rise and set, what stage the moon is in, which stars will be prominent, etc.

89

It comes from a Greek word that breaks into two parts: *epi-*, on or upon, and *hemera*, a day. So it's a list of what shall transpire in the sky upon a given day.

Q.   A program on the History Channel referred to the European Theater in World War II. Doesn't that seem a little bit flippant?

A.   I suppose it would be if it set out to demean the spectacle of war, but that's not the case. The Greek word that produced theater emphasized the sense of sight. For quite some time, it referred to the open-air structure where plays were presented to viewers.

One of the first English citations of the word shows up in Chaucer's *Boethius*: "Common strumpets of such a place that men call the theatre." By Shakespeare's day, the meaning had expanded to mean an area or region where something dramatic is open to public view, the scene of action.

The final step in the process came during World War I. A letter written by Winston Churchill in 1914 contained this: "The hand of war will I expect be heavy upon us in the Western Theatre during the next four weeks."

NOTE: a word about the spelling. Currently, theater is the American spelling, and theatre is the British spelling. In the 14th century, both spellings were acceptable. From 1550 to 1700, theater was prevalent. Somewhere in mid-18th century, the present arrangement clicked into place. One listener tried to make a distinction this way: theater is the spelling for movies and light entertainment, and theatre is preferred for classical plays and serious drama. There is no justification for this dichotomy.

Q.   One of my pet peeves is when people confuse lend and loan. It should be, "I need a loan. Lend me $100," not 'loan me $100.'

A.   Agreed—that is the current convention, though some dictionaries are willing to let "loan me" slide by in everything except formal writing.

This is a good example of something that I have said repeatedly: grammar and spelling conventions are temporary agreements at best. If they <u>can</u> change, they <u>will</u> change. That's built into the history of our language.

I sense that you see this as a recent abuse or deterioration of language, but you should know that 800 years ago, in 1200 a.d., *loan* as a verb began to appear in formal writing. Decrying the death of English is popular in some quarters, but the language will outlive its pallbearers.

Q. What can you tell me about eggcorns?

A. Eggcorn is the name given to misheard words or phrases, but only if the resulting error actually makes some sense. Contributors to the *Language Log* cooperatively invented the term after Mark Lieberman posted a note about the spelling egg corn being used in place of acorn. Here are some examples.

for all intensive purposes	for all intents and purposes
curve your enthusiasm	curb your enthusiasm
a pigment of your imagination	a figment of your imagination
antidotal evidence	anecdotal evidence
bare in mind	bear in mind
bedside manor	bedside manner
nip it in the butt	nip it in the bud
claim heartship	claim hardship
crutch of the matter	crux of the matter
death charge	depth charge
enact revenge	exact revenge
flaw in the ointment	fly in the ointment
time in memorial	time immemorial
on the spurt of the moment	on the spur of the moment

[For a full database, go to http://eggcorns.lascribe.net/]

Q. What I used to call a pry bar back home is called a crow bar around here. Why is that?

A. Originally (1400), it was called a crow, and the reason seems to be as simple as its shape. It's an iron bar with a wedge-shaped end, usually slightly bent and forked. Someone looked at it sideways and thought that it looked like a crow's head with a slightly opened beak.

Q. We all know the phrase "computer geek," but recently, I heard a commercial for a restaurant that claimed to have a "wine geek" on hand! A WINE GEEK!!! If I were a computer geek I would turn the tables (no pun intended) and market myself as a computer connoisseur!

A. No doubt about it—in my lifetime, the word geek has turned completely around so that now it is a folksy way of saying expert or connoisseur. What is absolutely delightful about this is that the word originally inspired horror and disgust. It referred to a performer in a carnival. His specialty act was meant to be bizarre, and it involved biting the heads off live chickens. Perhaps a wine geek removes the cork with his teeth.

Q. At what point do words become a solid piece of the language? Everyone knows *hola* and uses it on a regular basis, but it's still considered Spanish, whereas *defenestrate*, which comes from the French "fenetre," is considered an English word.

A. I don't think that there's a time rule for transference of foreign terms into English. When they stop being called foreign and are considered just as English as anything else can be a slow or a fast process. But I've noticed a few related things that take place.

- One is that they stop appearing in print with italics or quotation marks when they are finally welcomed into the club.
- They also eventually lose any accent marks that we don't use in English.
- Another sign is that they stop being defined in parentheses; they are simply accepted as familiar.
- Finally, when the assimilation process is complete, they will show up in an English dictionary filed alphabetically with all the other English words. An example would be bete noire. Those

QUICK QUIZ 18

Which one does not belong in this list?

(A) prurient (B) exemplary (C) salacious (D) lascivious

who know what it means treat it as if they were saying something like the bogeyman.

Other terms that have gone through this process include habeas corpus, genre, kimono, igloo, macho, heuristic, angst, gulag, klutz, paparazzi, and impasse.

Q. Where did cartoon come from?

A. We consider cartoons to be a form of entertainment, something humorous but ephemeral. In times gone by, cartoons served a far more serious purpose.

We find the base word *carta* in Latin, where it meant paper. As it was assimilated into Italian and French, it came to mean strong, heavy paper, a type of pasteboard. Rather than being covered with frivolous, inconsequential drawings, such pasteboard was used by serious artists to plot preliminary drawings of what were to become international masterpieces. Think of Da Vinci's notebooks.

If you've ever moved from one place to another without hiring a moving company, you've scurried around looking for a cartoon's close relative: cardboard cartons to be filled with your earthly possessions.

Q. I saw a reference to American soldiers fighting in World War I as doughboys. Why?

A. Referring to soldiers, the term goes back to the American Civil War. Before that, in 1685, doughboys were described as "cakes of bread." They seem to have been boiled, which would make them akin to dumplings.

Various explanations have been brought forth. One explanation, supported by General George Custer's widow, is that doughboys were small doughnuts served to sailors aboard ship, and the large brass buttons on infantry uniforms looked like them.

Another explanation is that it comes from the use of pipe clay dough to clean the infantrymen's white belts.

Q. Should it be an ex-president or a former president? Are the two interchangeable?

93

A.   This is one of the many manufactured controversies that bedevil people and make their lives unnecessarily complicated. Both *ex-* and *former* are properly used as designations for persons who have previously held the office in question.

H.W. Fowler seems to be the culprit in this case. His *A Dictionary of Modern English Usage* contains this entry for ex-: "For such patent yet prevalent absurdities as ex-Lord Mayor, ex-Chief Whip, ex-Tory Solicitor-General (except in another sense than its writer means), see HYPHENS; & for alternatives, LATE."

Fowler was often an elegant writer and a dispenser of common sense, but there was a spasm of personal preference in this entry disguised as proper grammar. Even he admits that saying *the late Lord Mayor* should be avoided "because of the doubt whether it means that the person's life, or his tenure of office, is over." In modern America, unless you are fond of using the phrase *of late* instead of the word *recently*, late means dead in this context.

I acknowledge that one of Fowler's points was to avoid ambiguous hyphenated terms, such as ex-Friend of the Library member. The single-minded among us could construe that to mean that this person is now a raving enemy of the library and a flaming book-burner, but the rest of us realize that ex- modifies the entire phrase, not simply the word to which it is attached.

So, many commentators have arrived at this compromise. (1) Use ex- for the immediate past office holder: ex-president George Bush. (2) Use former for all previous holders of the office: former president Jimmy Carter. (3) Use late to indicate a recently deceased holder of the office: the late president Gerald Ford.

Q.   What is hubris and how is the word used?

A.   It comes from a classical Greek term, and currently it means pride and excessive self-confidence.

ANSWER 18   (B) EXEMPLARY

Something exemplary is commendable and worthy of imitation. Prurient, salacious, and lascivious refer to things that pander to base instincts.

It was more than swollen ego in the old days. It was anger wrapped in insolence, and when it resulted in insulting, degrading treatment of another person, it was actually a crime. In Greek law, according to Liddell & Scott's *Greek-English Lexicon*, hubris included all the more serious injuries done to another, and it was a grievous assault. It could lead to public indictment.

When anger and contempt lead to lesser injuries upon another, Liddell and Scott say that it was known as *aikia*, and the remedy was more likely to be private action.

Variations on the word hubris historically included wantonness, lewdness, and restiveness on the part of overfed horses. I hate it when that happens.

Q. I heard a sportscaster say, "This is something you very rarely ever see". In a Hemingway moment of 'keep it simple', I asked myself if it could be better stated as, "This is something you rarely see". What purpose do the words "very" and "ever' serve?

A. Those words seem to have been added solely for emphasis. The combination of "very rarely" and "ever" is really a disguised but cautious way of saying "never," but without the 100% commitment.

The same thing happens with some pronouns, specifically the intensive and reflexive. "I saw it myself" gives no more information than "I saw it," but it adds emphasis. "I myself saw it" is the same packet of information, but placing *myself* directly behind *I* gives even more impact to the personal eye-witness nature of the statement.

So while you could shorten the original sentence and not lose the essential meaning, a rhetorical element would be lost.

Q. What is a sinking fund?

A. A sinking fund is a financial account into which deposits are made at intervals. Its purpose is to accumulate interest in order to reduce the principal of a debt. The British government established one in 1716.

In his *Commentaries on the laws of England* (1765–69), Sir William Blackstone explained the name: "The surpluses . . . are usually denominated the sinking fund, because originally destined to sink and lower the national debt."

95

Sidebar: a 2007 Michigan Senate bill proposed that the name "sinking fund" be changed to "infrastructure investment funds" in the ballot language of property tax millage increase requests. I guess the senator thought the original term was too negative.

Q. Where did "to have egg on your face" come from?

A. I'm still trying to figure out which came first, the chicken or the egg. To have egg on your face is to be embarrassed, to be humiliated, to look foolish. There is no agreement on the source, but the first of the following seems sensible.

- Some say it comes from the social situation in which you eat and inadvertently end up with food smeared on your face, the analog to spinach stuck in your teeth.
- Others say that it refers to actors pelted by eggs after a bad performance.
- Finally, there is a theory that it referred to egg-sucking dogs whose nefarious activities would be betrayed by the egg on their muzzles.

Q. I know that "out of the fold" means that someone is now outside an organization, a sort of outlaw, but where did it come from?

A. A fold is a fenced enclosure for domestic animals, especially sheep. It comes from the Old English *falaed*, an enclosed space. It is used as a metaphor for people united in belief or in common purpose. Thus, to be out of the fold is to abandon belief (if it's a voluntary act) or to be ostracized as a form of punishment or censure (if it's the group's decision).

Given the bucolic setting of the pre-Christian era, it's a favorite biblical term.

QUICK QUIZ 19

Which one does not belong in this list?

(A) torpor (B) acedia (C) indolence (D) robustness

•   Numbers 32:24 (KJV) "Build you cities for your little ones, and **fold**s for your sheep; and do that which hath proceeded out of your mouth."

•   Jeremiah 23:3 "And I will gather the remnant of my flock out of all countries whither I have driven them, and will bring them again to their **fold**s; and they shall be fruitful and increase."

•   In a spiritual sense, it reflects the concept of the Good Shepherd. "And other sheep I have, which are not of this fold: them also I must bring, and they shall hear my voice; and there shall be one fold, and one shepherd." [John 10:16]

It's also been used in secular settings.

•   *The Farmer's Law*, 8th c. Byzantium: "If a slave, while trying to steal by night, drives the sheep away from the flock in chasing them out of the fold, and they are lost or eaten by wild beasts, let him be hanged as a murderer."

•   It is better to keep the wolf out of the fold than to trust to drawing his teeth and talons after he shall have entered."— Thomas Jefferson, *notes on the State of Virginia*, c. 1781-1783.

Q.   What is a deadhead?

A.   The word covers a number of situations. The original deadhead (*caput mortuum*) was a word used in alchemy to refer to the residue left after a substance was distilled. It was useless, good for nothing but disposal. Perhaps some of that transferred to deadhead, but there was also the idea that when it came to counting heads to determine profit, the deadhead was getting a free ride and would be counted without contributing.

A **Deadhead** may refer to:

•   A commercial carrier with no paying passengers or freight. It is simply returning to base.

•   Similarly, it sometimes is used as a verb to describe a taxicab driving some distance without a paying passenger.

•   In the airline industry, it's a flight crew member (either flight attendant or pilot) who is in uniform traveling on a scheduled flight, but not working that flight, Essentially, that crew member is being repositioned to work from a different city.

•   In the early part of the nineteenth century the term *dead head* (at first two words) was a theatrical term for a person who had been admitted without charge, perhaps because they had performed some service such as putting up a poster advertising the event.

• A deadhead was a loyal fan of the long-running musical group *The Grateful Dead*. It joins a set of insult words ending in *-head*, such as pothead, crackhead, airhead, butthead, cheesehead, egghead, and so on.

Q. When should I use *speak* and when should I use *talk*?

A. There's actually not much practical difference between them, although *talk* might be a little less formal.

However, when it comes to idioms using these words, there will be a distinction.
• "She speaks (not *talks*) four languages fluently."
• "You talk (not *speak*) too much."
• "His behavior speaks (not *talks*) volumes."
• "Speak (not *talk*) your mind."
• "I can't stand it when you talk (not *speak*) behind my back."
• "There's a problem; we need to talk (not *speak*)."
• "He talks (not *speaks*) in his sleep."

Q. The word "rakish" was used in a local paper to describe a border collie. I thought rakish meant sexy looks, not so much distinctive.

A. The primary definition of a rake (the person) is someone of loose, immoral, and dissipated habits, so the adjective rakish attached to such a person would have a negative connotation.

The problem comes from the fact that there is a separate "rakish" used as a nautical term. There, it means having a trim, streamlined appearance. It's used as a synonym for dashing and jaunty. That's pushing it for a dog that looks like it's wearing clown makeup, but perhaps we can ascribe it to journalistic enthusiasm.

ANSWER 19   (D) ROBUSTNESS

Robustness involves sturdiness and strong activity.

Torpor, acedia, and indolence involve laziness and inactivity.

Q. I know a bow is something in a girl's hair. It is curvy (the bow that is). A bow is a weapon that is also curved. So I figured the word bow, as in to "bow to the queen," must also mean something curvy. So why is one pronounced *bau* and the other *boe*?

A. You're on to something with your observation. The original "bow" seems to have been a Danish word that signified a bend in the river. Elbow and rainbow are cousins. Although both words have the same spelling, they come from two different sources, each with different pronunciations. Bow (to bend over, *bau*) originally sounded something like *boo*, and bow (the weapon, *boe*) sounded like *boe*.

Q. I've been reading about "speaking in tongues". Is this a language? Do the syllables mean anything? Maybe it's a touchy subject for radio.

A. It might be touchy if I got into theology, but I'll stick with linguistics. The technical term is glossolalia (or xenoglossia), and it is a phenomenon that may take place during religious ecstasy. The words spoken are usually meaningless syllables. This has been confirmed by recordings examined by language experts. The sounds reflect the primary language of the person uttering the syllables; that is, the glossolalia of people from Poland, Spain, and the United States all sound quite different from each other, but resemble the sounds of the Polish, Spanish, and American English languages, respectively.

It all goes back to the Pentecost account found in *The Acts of the Apostles*, Chapter 2:

³ And there appeared unto them cloven tongues like as of fire, and it sat upon each of them.

⁴ And they were all filled with the Holy Ghost, and began to speak with other tongues, as the Spirit gave them utterance.

Q. Is there a connection between the word naught and the word naughty?

A. There is. The word naughty is a rather insipid word these days. We use it to describe the mischievous infractions of children, the accidents of our pets, or as a synonym for saucy. But in the 15th and 16th centuries, it was a word used to describe industrial-strength wickedness. It ranged from morally evil to turpitudinous to licentious.

One element of the word naught started as the word no and its variants in Scandinavian, Old High German, Frisian and Saxon. It had the force of not, in no way, by no means. So the earlier version of naughty described a person who had no ethical standards or qualms, who in no way was a good person.

An alternate spelling (still used in Britain) is nought, but American English seems to prefer naught.

Q. Why does "take a powder" mean get out of here?

A. "Take a powder!" used to be a more popular saying. It was a gruff demand that the targeted person leave. No one seems to know with certainty how the phrase started, but that never squelches speculation.

In 17th century Britain, the colloquial verb *to powder* meant to rush, to hurry impetuously. "Zacheus climb'd the Tree: But O how fast. . . (when Our Saviour called) he powder'd down agen!" [1632, Francis Quarles, *Divine Fancies*, I. lxvii]

Around the same time, *to dust* was a colloquial American phrase meaning to ride or go quickly, hasten, hurry, make off. "Stick thou To thy sure trot..Let folly dust it on, or lag behind." [1655, Henry Vaughan, *Silex Scintillans*, I. Rules & Lessons]

But it wasn't until 1916 that we see Americans using *to take a powder*: "Look at the two birds trying to take a run-out powder on the eats." [1916, Washington Post, May 20] Four years later, we find this: "The 'Wilmington' challenged us to a boat race, but when we slapped up a sack of good Chinese taels [money] to back our team, the 'Wily Willie' took a run-out powder and called off the race." [1920, *Our Navy*, Aug. 33/1]

Notice that in both cases, the form is *to take a run-out powder*. Powdered medicines were common in that era for anything that ailed you, so it is vaguely possible that the origin of the phrase was a reference to a mythical medicine that would grant you speed. But there was a pejorative edge to the phrase.

Over the years, many explanations have been proffered:
- it started as a reference to gunpowder, which explosively propels bullets and shells.
- it's a reference to a laxative powder, which would cause you to move quickly to the nearest toilet.
- it's a reference to the dust that our feet raise when we are scampering off. (This has become a cartoon stereotype.)

- it's a reference to the "magical" powder used by magicians to make things disappear.

Q. I came across a reference to a blind pig. In context, it sounds like it means a speakeasy. Is that correct?

A. That's close. A speakeasy (popular during Prohibition) was an establishment that served liquor when it was totally illegal to do so. A blind pig often sold liquor by the shot glass in an area where it was legal only in closed containers in larger quantities (pints, quarts, gallons). In other cases, the operators of a blind pig were simply avoiding the licensing fees that would be required for a saloon.

The whole thing was based on a transparent ruse. You would pay your money to see "a blind pig" or some other exotic animal. When you stepped up to the window or the hole in the wall, a "free" glass of liquor would be waiting for you.

Minnesota passed a law against blind pigs in 1887: "Whoever shall attempt to evade or violate any of the laws of this state...by means of the artifice or contrivance known as the "Blind Pig" or "Hole in the Wall"...shall...be punished."

In the South, the same concept was called a blind tiger. "I sees a kinder pigeon-hole cut in the side of a house, and over the hole, in big writin', 'Blind Tiger, ten cents a sight.' Says I to the feller inside, 'here's your ten cents. Walk out your wild cat.' I'll be dodbusted if he didn't shove out a glass of whiskey. You see, that blind tiger was an arrangement to evade the law, which won't let them sell likker there." [*Spirit of the Times*, 1857]

Q. A recent headline in the *Traverse City Record-Eagle* proclaimed, "Local man plans to get back on his soap box." This prompted some questions on the origin of *soap box*.

A. First of all, there's the word soap. In a reversal of the usual historical direction, it seems to have worked its way into Latin as *sapo*. Originally, it came from Teutonic or Tartar languages.

Literally, a soap box was a wooden crate used to deliver soap. Empty, it made a convenient platform to raise a speaker slightly above his audience so that he might be seen and heard. Since many of these public speakers embraced eccentric or quirky ideas, and since they usually employed a passionate style of oratory, *to get on your soapbox* took on a pejorative cast.

The *soapbox derby* was so named because a wooden crate often formed the riding compartment of the vehicle. (Derby is the name of an English town where a famous horse race was held annually.)

Q.   Where did the word eavesdrop come from?

A.   Today it means to secretly listen in on a conversation. It's an Old English word going back to at least the 9th century. The eaves of a house is the projecting overhang at the lower edge of a roof. Water drips from it when it rains.

An Old English law mandated that the owner of a building must leave at least two feet from the boundary of his property open to the sky. This was so water dripping from the roof line did not erode the neighbor's land or damage his buildings. The Romans had similar laws on their books, called *iura stillicidiorum*, or *laws of the falling drops*. [Chambers-Murray, *Latin-English Dictionary*]

By extension, the eavesdrip was the space between the dripping water line and the wall of the house. An eavesdropper would be someone who crept close to a door or window to listen in on a conversation.

"Evesdroppers are such as stand under wals or windowes..to heare news." [*Termes de la Ley*, 1641]

Q.   When we want a coffee, many old timers will say, "Gimme a cuppa joe." Why is joe a synonym for coffee?

A.   No one knows with certainty, but here's how I stitch it together from various sources. Jamoke or jamocha was slang concocted by tramps and hoboes. It first appears in 1914: " There ain't nothin' better in th' booze line than pure alky mixed with jamocha." [P & T Casey, *The Gay Cat*]

QUICK QUIZ 20

Which one does not belong in this list?

(A) caustic   (B) mordant   (C) ingratiating   (D) sardonic

The word jamocha was a blend of Java and Mocha, two places known for the best coffee. Joe was a shortened or clipped form of jamocha.

Early examples are particularly common from U.S. Navy sources. From Lt. Robert Erdman's 1931 *Reserve Officer's Manual*: "Jamoke, Java, Joe. Coffee. Derived from the words Java and Mocha, where originally the best coffee came from..."

Q.   What is the difference between an engine and a motor?

A.   I received help on this one from a listener who is an engineer. In short, according to him, a motor is electrical-driven; an engine is fuel-driven.

In everyday, non-technical usage the words have much the same meaning. The IEEE *Spectrum magazine* for June 1998 argues that the difference is that engines contain their own fuel or are part of a highly integrated engine-fuel system, whereas a motor draws on externally supplied energy. In other words, engines consume their fuel; motors don't.

However, thanks to loose popular terminology, there are some anomalies. Motor oil should actually be engine oil. A motor boat should be an engine boat. But who's counting?

Q.   I sometimes have trouble telling when to use *past* and when to use *passed*.

A.   This is a problem that comes up only when you are writing. When you are speaking, since *past* and *passed* are homophones, they will sound alike.

If you are referring to time or distance, use "past":
• The team performed well in the past.
• The police car drove past the suspect's house.
• She has a shady past

If you are referring to the action of *passing,* however, you need to use "passed":
• When John passed the gravy, he spilled it on his lap.
• The teacher was astonished that none of the students had passed the test.
• The pain subsided when he passed a kidney stone.

Q. What's the difference between nil and null?

A. First, they have different origins. Nil comes from the Latin *nihil*, which meant nothing. Null came from the Latin *nullus*, which meant non-existent.

Nil tends to be used in reference to quantity, where it means zero or no amount. Null often shows up in reference to quality, where it means void, inefficacious, or invalid.

Q. A listener inquired about the word *proactive*, commenting that logically, it should mean "in favor of activity."

A. Let's cover the meaning first, then get back to the prefix *pro-*, which has more than one meaning.

The word *proactive* was used by logotherapy's founder, Victor Frankl, in his book *Man's Search for Meaning*. He meant it as an antonym to *reactive*. In his view, mentally healthy people do not simply react to external circumstances. Rather, they act according to what they see as meaningful in their lives no matter what is happening externally.

In non-clinical use, the word means taking initiative, anticipating events, and controlling a situation rather than indulging in a series of knee-jerk reactions.

Let's get back to the prefix *pro-*. It can mean *in favor of*, as in the words pro-American, pro-business, or pro-war. But it can also mean *towards the front* (proclaim, propose), *in anticipation of* (proactive, provide), *onward or forward* (proceed, progress), or, especially in science, *a precursor* (pro-agonic, prohormone).

The lesson is this: don't wed yourself to just one meaning for this prefix. Let context help you sort out which meaning is involved, or reach for that handy dictionary.

ANSWER 20   (C) INGRATIATING

INGRATIATING MEANS PLEASANT AND AGREEABLE.
Caustic, mordant, and sardonic refer to unpleasant and sarcastic comments.

Q.   A trailer is something that you attach to the rear bumper of your car, and if someone is trailing in a race, she has fallen behind. Yet, when it comes to movies, the trailer comes *before* the feature film. Why the name?

A.   In the old days, movies were shown in a continuous loop and audiences were allowed to sit through multiple showings of the same movie—the start times were published and if you came in late you simply sat through the next showing until you came to the point "where you came in."

The coming attractions reel would be spliced onto the end of the last reel of the movie, hence the name trailer. From the perspective of the audience member who arrived on time or a little early, the coming attractions would appear before the feature, even though technically it was at the end.

If there was only one feature, the projectionist would stop right after the credits. When he started it up again, the last part of the reel—the trailer—would appear to be the first part. Advertising filmmakers didn't want to lose a captive audience.

The term dates to the 1920s. From the *New York Times* of 11 March 1928: "A trailer, a few hundred feet of film announcing a forthcoming picture."

Q.   I came across a strange word recently – caterwauling. It seemed to mean complaining or whining.

A.   That's where it has settled now, but it was louder in the old days: the screeching of cats.

This word has two components. The first part, *cater-*, contains the word cat. While there seems to be some uncertainty, the German word *kater*, a tomcat, probably had some influence. The word shows up in a colorful idiom: *einen kater haben*, to have a hangover.

The second component is more traceable. It comes from the verb *wrawen*, to wail or howl. The word was used in reference to cats in heat, and it may simply have been onomatopoeia, an imitation of the sound itself. Other language groupings such as Danish, Swedish, Norwegian, and Swiss, had similar words referring to cats in heat, and the word also applied to stallions in heat and to a rowdy, poorly behaved man.

So the earliest use of the word was to describe the noise made by cats at rutting time. Later, it came to mean any hideous noise or a quarrel in feline fashion. It also meant lascivious or lecherous.

Q.   Is there a difference between seasonal and seasonable?

A.   Some people still try to maintain a distinction. Seasonal means pertaining to a particular season.
- The store has seasonal variations in opening times, and it is closed in January.
- There's a seasonal rise in school enrollment every September.
- He suffers from seasonal affect disorder.

Seasonable applies to what is <u>appropriate</u> to a season.
- She wore seasonable clothing, including a woolen scarf.
- The sun is shining and the temperature is seasonable for spring.
- Christmas carols are seasonable in December.

Q.   Where did "kick the bucket" come from?

A.   The stereotype cartoon has a cowboy stretched out on the ground after a gunfight, a wooden bucket near his feet. One final spasm and he kicks the bucket, or dies. Perhaps it's the water pouring out of the bucket that is meant to be a symbol of the life force pouring out of him.

The problem is that there are two words bearing the spelling *bucket*, and as the *Oxford English Dictionary* comments, it is uncertain which word is related to the proverbial saying. It does provide a citation, however, that might be enough to tip the balance: "The beam on which a pig is suspended after he has been slaughtered is called in Norfolk, even in the present day, a 'bucket'. Since he is suspended by his heels, the phrase to 'kick the bucket' came to signify to die." [*Mod. Newspaper*]

QUICK QUIZ 21

Which one does not belong in this list?

(A) sanguine (B) morose (C) lugubrious (D) disconsolate

I had the misfortune of visiting a pork slaughterhouse in the days when the Chicago Stockyards were still in operation, and I can testify to the violent thrashing, kicking, and squealing that hogs are capable of in their final moments.

Q.   Is "the pot calling the kettle black" a racist comment of some sort?

A.   Absolutely not. It goes back to an earlier time when cooking was a much dirtier and messier task. When you cook over burning logs, carbon is a by-product, and it coats the cooking utensils over time, turning them black. There's not much sense in scrubbing the outside of the pots and pans because they'll just start turning black again the next time you put them on the fire.

So the pot calling the kettle black means that you are accusing someone of a misdemeanor of which you yourself are guilty. Since both containers have been over the same fire, the pot is just as soot-covered as the kettle.

Brewer's *Dictionary of Phrase and Fable* matches this with a French proverb: "The shovel mocks the poker." Again, both implements would be equally stained from poking logs and removing coals and ashes.

Q.   Is sycophant a fancy term for a brown nose?

A.   Indeed it is. In a spasm of synonyms, the *Oxford English Dictionary* flings this at us: "A mean, servile, cringing, or abject flatterer; a parasite, toady, lickspittle."

But its origin is a bit mysterious. Some early citations imply that the original sycophants were informants who ratted on merchants engaged in illegal fig trading (the *syco-* root means fig in Greek).

A competing theory says that it refers to the obscene gesture called "showing the fig," which consisted of pushing the thumb between two fingers and holding them up. It embodies the same contemptuous intent embedded in thrusting the middle finger straight up in the air as a display.

Q.   What is the origin of the naval term "aye, aye, Sir"?

A. "Aye, aye, Sir" is the standard response for a sailor to give to a superior. As Charles from Atwood confirmed in his call-in, the double aye is meant to convey that the order has been both received *and* understood.

There is some confusion over the origin of the term, however, probably because there are two ayes. One of them meant forever or always; the other meant yes. There is some speculation that the latter came from the former, the transition being something like always/by all means/with certainty/yes. [*Oxford English Dictionary*]

But militating against this is the fact that the first written instances spell that version of yes as I:

- "If you say I, syr, we will not say no." [1576, *Tyde Taryeth no Man*]
- "Nothing but No and I, and I and No." [1594, Drayton, *Idea*, 57]

At various times it was also spelled ey, ai, ay, and hye. So the suggestion found on some web sites that aye is an initialism for "at your [service] ever" lacks any foundation.

Q. I'm intrigued by the phrase "strapped for cash." The image that pops into my mind is someone whose hands are strapped behind his back, thus making it impossible for him to reach for his wallet.

A. I like the image, but that doesn't seem to be its origin. It's a bit hazy, but here's what I've been able to stitch together. The phrase started in the mid-19th century, and it meant short of cash.

Earlier in that century, *strap* was a slang term for credit. When you bought something on credit, the seller kept a tally by notching the stick that represented your account. While the balance was still due, the merchant had plenty of strap, but no cash.

Here's a quote from 1876: "Meal and milk. . .were had from the neighbouring farmhouses, and in reckoning for the latter a system of 'strap' then existed which was easily checked by both buyer and

---

ANSWER 21   (A) SANGUINE

Sanguine means cheerful and optimistic.

Morose, lugubrious, and disconsolate denote gloom and sadness.

seller. This was done by what was called a 'milk stick'." [*Round about Bradford*]

Q. Why do we call a boxing ring a ring when it's actually square, and how did tennis courts and basketball courts get to be called *courts*?

A. Originally, the bystanders formed a large circle around the fighters; that was the ring. Here's an illustration from 1659: "The soldyers generally say they will not fight, but will make a ring for their officers to fight in." [*Clarke Papers*]

Sports courts are called that because "court" was once a synonym for quadrangle. Thus, a courtyard was a rectangular yard attached to the king's residence. To this day, the venue for basketball or tennis is a rectangular surface.

Q. Should it be preventative or preventive? I've heard both of them used, but that seems redundant.

A. This one is a bit thorny. Conservative commentators such as Bryan Garner (*Modern American Usage*) huff and puff about preventative: "The strictly correct form is preventive (as both noun and adjective) though the corrupt form with the extra internal syllable is unfortunately common."

Then there are those with a longer memory of history, such as *Merriam-Webster's Concise Dictionary of English Usage*: "The critics have panned preventative for over a century, preferring its shorter synonym preventive in spite of the fact that both words have been around for over 300 years and both have had regular use by reputable writers."

The first instance of preventive given by the *Oxford English Dictionary* is by Francis Bacon in 1626. The first citation for preventative is from Roger Boyle Orrery in 1655.

The conclusion? Neither one is a corruption, but many contemporary grammarians favor the shorter version.

Q. I'm curious about the origin of the word **public** and whether its meaning has changed over the years.

A. Currently, it means open to general view. In the last few hundred years, the meaning has vacillated between "the opposite of private" and "representing the community."

It came from the Latin word *pubes*, an adult male. In the days of ancient Rome, something public was done for the state or at the expense of the state. In the long run, the biggest shift has been from emphasis on the state to emphasis on the citizen.

Q. This sentence appeared in our local paper: "Conducting [music] is a sort of nepharious art. It's difficult to get across the different skills that are involved . . ."

A. Obviously, the reporter spelled the word nepharious according to sound; it should be nefarious. But something else emerges when you consider the entire quote: "'Conducting [music] is a sort of nepharious art. It's difficult to get across the different skills that are involved,' [Frank Almond] said, adding that he needed to master rehearsal organization and communication without speaking as well as learn the score from different perspectives."

Nefarious means extremely wicked, so it's totally out of place here. The context shows that **nebulous** was the word needed—vague, indistinct, without exact boundaries, lacking precise rules.

Q. I'm wondering if "used to" is a real verb.

A. *Used to* is a real verb form. The only problem with the form occurs in speech, where people tend to slur it into "useta."

"Used to" expresses the idea that something was an old habit that ended in the past. It indicates that something was often repeated in the past, but it is not usually done now. [*I used to smoke.*]

"Used to" can also be employed to talk about past generalizations that are no longer true. [*People used to think that the earth was flat.*]

QUICK QUIZ 22

Which one does not belong in this list?

(A) tautology (B) paucity (C) redundancy (D) pleonasm

Q. I was watching an old crime movie last night, and one of the characters said, "I gotta fence some goods." I know it means to sell some loot, but why fence?

A. The verb **fence** is usually connected with protection and disguise, thus reinforcing the idea of ill-gotten goods being concealed. "To fence property, to sell anything that is stolne." [1610, *Martin Mark-all, beadle of Bridewell, his defence and answere to the belman of London*]

The noun **fence**, meaning a receiver of stolen goods, is recorded in *Memoirs of John Hall*, 4th edition, 1708: "Fence, one that buys stoln goods." It seems to be connected to a literal fence, a barrier to hide and protect things. Ultimately, it is connected to the word defense.

Q. How did "so long" come to mean goodbye?

A. It has the impact of "so long as it takes to see you again." Our modern version is "see you later." There are similar idioms in German and Scandinavian.

After some research, I discovered that it was once rather exotic to the educated classes in America because it was a phrase used by the lower classes. Walt Whitman popularized it in *Leaves of Grass* [1855]:

> An unknown sphere, more real than I dream'd, more direct, darts
> awakening rays about me—So long!
> Remember my words—I may again return,
> I love you—I depart from materials;
> I am as one disembodied, triumphant, dead.

Whitman's friend William Sloane Kennedy, wrote in 1923: "The salutation of parting—'So long!'—was, I believe, until recent years, unintelligible to the majority of persons in America, especially in the interior, and to members of the middle and professional classes. I had never heard of it until I read it in *Leaves of Grass*, but since then have quite often heard it used by the laboring class and other classes in New England cities. Walt wrote to me, defining 'so long' thus: 'A salutation of departure, greatly used among sailors, sports, & prostitutes—the sense of it is 'Till we meet again,'— conveying an inference that somehow they will doubtless so meet, sooner or later."

NOTE: Listener Jim Dalyrimple points out that in many languages, there are two ways to say goodbye. One is permanent; the other is temporary. In some cultures, the distinction needs to be kept.

Q.   In baseball, we have a bullpen. Where did that come from?

A.   What I know with certainty is that the original bullpen was an enclosure for bulls. Later it evolved into a prison for humans, then into any enclosure or confining space. How it came to be applied to the relief pitchers' waiting area is a matter of speculation.

•   Tim McCarver claims that it came from an on-air announcer who said, "They look like bulls waiting to be let out of a pen," referring to the relief pitchers.

•   Another story says that manager Casey Stengel suggested that the term came from managers who were fed up with relievers "shootin' the bull" during games, so they were given a "bullpen" away from other players.

•   There's also the theory that the term dates to the very early days of baseball when fans were herded like cattle into a standing room only area.

•   Finally, Moe Berg claimed that the relief pitchers were always behind a billboard, and the principal sponsor was Bull Durham chewing tobacco.

Choose your pitch.

Q.   I came across the word sweatmeat. I have no idea what it means, but it sounds absolutely disgusting.

A.   Ah, the idiosyncrasies of spelling. That was an early way to spell sweetmeat. Early on, meat was a synonym for food in general and an antonym of drink. Sweetmeat was sweet pastry, confectionary, or candied fruit and nuts.

Q.   Not to be indelicate, but where did the word poop come from?

ANSWER 22   (B) PAUCITY

Paucity involves economy of expression, few words.

Tautology, redundancy, and pleonasm involve needless repetition.

A.   Originally, in Chaucer, to poop was to produce a short blast of sound on a horn. By 1869, it was being used as slang and as a child's euphemism for farting: "To poop, from the Belgian *poepen*, to fart softly: both from the sound." [*Gazophylacium Anglicanum*, 1689]

Q.   I'm a 5th grader at Immaculate Conception, and we listen to your program during our Tuesday English class. While playing balderdash, I came across the word wallydrag. Where did that come from?

A.   Welcome aboard, class. As you know from playing the game, it now refers to the runt of the litter. When it became implanted in English in 1508, it had a mean edge to it: "a feeble, ill-grown person or animal; a worthless, slovenly person, esp. a woman." [Blame the *Oxford English Dictionary*, not me.]
        It breaks into two parts. "Wally" meant an unfashionable person, and "to draggle" was to pull something through the dirt.

Q.   Shouldn't there be a word *overneath* to act as opposite to *underneath*?

A.   Inquiring minds want to know. This would be a logical antonym except for one thing: in Old English, *nethen* meant beneath, so underneath is really a hidden redundancy (under the beneath). The *be-* in beneath is an intensifier, not a simple declaration of existence.

Q.   Where does "mama" come from as a baby's word for mother?

A.   The prevailing theory is that it is connected to breastfeeding and the lip-smacking response that a suckling infant makes, but don't forget that English-speaking parents tend to refer to themselves as mommy and daddy.
        For the first few months of life, all the words that we direct at an infant go right over its head. It hears the sounds and begins to perceive patterns after thousands of repetitions (a necessary step in wiring their little brains for a specific language), but it makes as much sense to them as a ticking clock.
        The first thing that snaps into place for most babies is that these two primary creatures are intimately and invariably connected to certain

sounds. At that moment, the link is made between sound and sense, and language comprehension begins.

Oddly enough, in most languages mother is represented by a word with the letter *–m-*, and father often turns out to sound something like *dada, papa,* or *tata.*

Q   Why does "to have someone over a barrel" mean to have someone at your mercy?

A.   Again, there are choices. One explanation is that drowning victims were resuscitated by gently rolling them over a barrel, face down, to expel the water from their lungs. They were in a helpless position.

The other one refers to the posture assumed for punishment. This is alluded to in an 1869 poem by Brick Pomeroy titled *Nonsense*:

> I'd like to be a school-marm,
> And with the school-marms stand,
> With a bad boy over a barrel
> And with a spanker in my hand

Q.   Why do we say dead reckoning when we talk about determining position? What's dead about it?

A.   That particular meaning for dead also shows up in terms such as dead right, dead wrong, dead ahead, and dead last. There, as in dead reckoning, it means absolutely and completely. It has nothing to do with loss of life.

Dead reckoning is a fallback position in navigation. To use it, you must know your speed, your direction of travel, and the time elapsed since your last known position.

It is not as secure as pilotage (using visible landmarks), celestial navigation (using stars and planets), or electronic equipment (using satellites), but it is a lifesaving Plan B.

Q.   I've begun to notice a lot of words ending in –aholic. Where did that come from?

A.   They are all based on a single word –alcoholic—and they share a common meaning: addicted to something named in the first half of the word. Thus, we have chocaholic, newsaholic, spendaholic, sugarholic, and so on.

This urge to create humorous terms from an existing word pops up periodically. Watergate led to Irangate, Plamegate, Whitewatergate, Camillagate, Billygate, and uncounted others.

Q. To have a serious division of opinion is "to be at loggerheads." What's wood got to do with it?

A. Many attribute it to the loggerhead, an iron instrument with a long handle and a metal ball or bulb at the end used, when heated in the fire, for melting pitch and for heating liquids. It may have been used as a weapon by irate sailors.

The wood connection comes from the original meaning of the word: a blockhead.

Q. I'm looking for information on the phrase, "coin of the realm."

A. In its literal sense, it meant the legal currency of a given political unit. In its early existence, the word coin had multiple spellings, all deriving from a Latin word meaning corner or wedge [*cuneus*]. The coin was struck with a wedge-shaped device holding a die that imprinted image and inscription on a blank disc. In time, the word transferred from the die to the money itself. After many centuries, the spelling *coin* is now reserved for the money, and *quoin* has been allocated to the corner, angle, or wedge.

Ultimately, the phrase *coin of the realm* developed into a figurative sense: something valued or used as if it were money in a particular sphere. Here are some diverse examples:
- "Fear, of course, has been the coin of the realm for oppressive and dictatorial governments throughout history. Frighten the citizenry and they'll practically beg you to take away their freedom." [*Future of Freedom Foundation*]
- "Latte is the coin of the realm." [*Joseph Gallivan*]
- "Credibility is the coin of the realm." [*Dana Blankenhorn*, quoting George Schultz]
- "Scholarly books are the coin of the realm of knowledge." [*Peter Givler*]

• "Information is the coin of the realm in the capital."
[*Eloise Salholz*]
• "On the web, English has become the coin of the realm."
[*WSJ.com*]
• "The MBA generally is recognized as the coin of the realm for graduate business education." [*Stanley Gabor*]

Q. Why is "John Q. Public" used as a generic name for the common man?

A. John has been the common generic name for a male for centuries. John Q. Public was invented specifically to designate an American citizen.

As for the Q. as a middle initial, this information from *Notes & Queries* is useful: "John Citizen. . .is not so frequent in American usage as John Q. Public. . . It is probably a play on the name of an early president, John Q(uincy) Adams. [6 Mar. 1937, 177/2]

Q. Hodgepodge seems to mean a mess, a jumble. Is that correct?

A. That's about right—it is a heterogeneous mixture, though not necessarily always in a bad sense. Originally, it was a dish made from different kinds of meats and vegetables stewed together. In English law, it was the blending of properties in order to facilitate equal distribution.

It's a blend in itself: the French *hocher*, to shake together, and the English *pot*, a container.

Q. What is a stumblebum?

A. It's a slang term for a punch-drunk boxer, and, by extension, anyone who is clumsy, inept, and awkward. By 1932, it had come to

---

QUICK QUIZ 23

Which one does not belong in this list?

(A) furtive (B) manifest (C) surreptitious (D) clandestine

mean an alcoholic. Hemingway used the word in *Death in the Afternoon*: "The American word would be awkward bum, stumble-bum, flat-footed tramp."

As for its origin, it probably came from the Norwegian *stumla*, to grope and stumble in the dark.

Q. Jim Cramer of CNBC spoke of a certain company's habit of "kitchen sinking" their financial reports. Do you know what that means?

A. To kitchen sink is to announce all of a company's bad financial news at one time. A company deliberately overloads a report or press conference to overwhelm the reader/listener.
- "In the banking sector, UBS rallied from opening lows to add 2.62 pct as investors cheered the group's attempt to **kitchen sink** its subprime exposure." [*Thompson Financial News*]
- "There is a general feeling on both Wall Street and Main Street that the financials attempted to bottle up all of their losses in one bad quarter. They tried **to 'kitchen sink'** the bit." [Jutia Group: *Market Jitters & Political Critters*]
- "There's a whole chapter in the Hite book on unfair tactics men use in fights ... withdrawal, ridicule, teasing, emotional violence. But there's no mention of the classic female tactics ... like **"kitchen-sinking"**, where she drags in ammunition from every battle they have ever fought, dredging her elephantine memory for past hurts, never-forgotten sins he once committed. [Bettina Arndt, "Are men really so terrible?" *Sun Herald*, November 8, 1987]

Q. When I am sending email I often come across this dilemma. Evaluate the following sentence: "I was wondering if you have plans for dinner." This sentence does not contain a question mark because it is not phrased as a question. If I had said, "Do you have plans for dinner?" I would expect to put a question mark in there. Am I correct?

A. You are right about that question mark. It is used only when a direct question is written; an indirect question gets a period.

Did you know that your shoelace is untied?

I wonder if you know that your shoelace is untied.

A direct question wants to know something; an indirect question wants to report something.

Q.   I heard a reference to a "tobacco non-user" the other day on your station. It sounds so awkward and indirect. What's wrong with the people who write ads?

A.   I suppose it's an extension of non-smoker or the like, and it is a bit awkward. On the other hand, it's not some kind of modern corruption. Back in 1881, this appeared: "The average life of drunkards is only thirty-five years and six months. The average life of non-users, on the other hand, is sixty-four." [*Princeton Reverie*, Jan.-June 1881, p. 89]

Q.   Isn't bric-a-brac just another word for junk?

A.   Don't let your wife overhear you. Like mine, she may have this as her working motto: "One person's junk is another person's treasure." Bric-a-brac is defined as "old curiosities of artistic character" by the *Oxford English Dictionary*. Allegedly, it comes from a French phrase meaning by hook or by crook.
       This question led to other collector words on that program.

- bauble: a showy trinket [OF *baubel*, child's toy]
- gewgaw: a trifle [1225 *Ancren Riwle*, possibly >OE form of give, ca. 831]
- knickknack:, a toy, trinket, trifle. [reduplication of knack, 1540]
- trinket: A trifling ornament or toy; a trinket, bauble, knick-knack; hence pl,, small and trifling articles, [>trick, 1553]
- tsatske/tchotchke/chachka: a trinket or gewgaw [1964 Yiddish —Polish dialectical *czaczka*]

ANSWER 23   (B) MANIFEST

Manifest means open or apparent to the sight.

Furtive, surreptitious, and clandestine all mean hidden or secret.

Q.   Why does "behind the eight ball" mean in trouble?

A.   It's a metaphor from a certain type of pool game. The balls are numbered and must be pocketed in order. Since the eight ball can be pocketed only after all the other balls are gone, the game is forfeited if a player's cue ball hits the black (eight ball) first. A "behind the eight ball" position leaves a player in imminent danger of losing.

Q.   I remember this banter from my childhood, and I have heard it since.

Statement: *Did not!*   (short for "I did not do what you said I did.")

Response: *Did too!*   (short for some form of "Yes you did.")
This continues until one sibling runs out of breath. I have two questions: what does "to/two/too" perform for the argument, and which spelling is correct?

A.   The spelling you're looking for is *too*. It's an adverb, and normally it means "in addition" or "besides." But in this one case, where two people are on opposite sides of an argument ("Did NOT!"/"Did TOO!"), it is used as a word of emphasis.

I checked it out in the *Oxford English Dictionary*, and it turns out to be an American invention. It shows up first in print in Booth Tarkington's novel *Penrod*, 1914. So it's not all that old as far as usages go. But anyone who grew up with a brother or sister got a lot of use from it.

Q.   I have an oldie for you: 23 skidoo.

A.   This was something that flappers would say as they scampered out of the room. Skidoo was probably a variant of skedaddle, meaning to depart in haste. It was a slang term used during the American Civil War, and may have developed from scatter or scuttle.

The 23 is a problem. One persistent explanation found on the internet is that 23 was telegrapher's code for "be gone with you." But I found some Morse code charts from that period that clearly show that 23 was code for "this message is for all stations."

After that, the explanations are worthy of a novelist:

- Twenty-Third Street in New York City was the location of many railroad and ferry depots, so people were constantly taking their leave.
- A certain racetrack had room for 22 horses in the starting gate. A 23rd horse had to line up behind them, and would have to run like blazes to stand any chance of winning.
- In Charles Dickens' *Tale of Two Cities*, hero Sydney Carton is 23rd in line to be executed at the guillotine. The peasant women who are sitting there knitting count off the numbers as the heads roll. "The murmuring of many voices, the upturning of many faces, the pressing on of many footsteps in the outskirts of the crowd, so that it swells forward in a mass, like one great heave of water, all flashes away. Twenty-Three."

Adding a bit of likelihood to the last explanation is that around the time that 23 skidoo took hold (1899), *Tale of Two Cities* was being presented as a very popular play. But there's nothing definitive.

Q. Why is an informant called a snitch?

A. It has a strange little story to tell. Snitch started as a stroke or a tap against the nose with a finger flipped off the thumb [1676]. Then it meant the nose itself [1700]. Finally, it meant an informer, one who turns King's or Queen's evidence.

Not coincidentally, nose was slang for a spy or informer, especially for the police. The moral: don't stick your nose where it's not wanted.

Q. ABC news had a story during the week telling of a storm that "plundered the west coast." Do you think they meant "pummeled"?

A. Absolutely. Plunder is what a pirate does: rob, pillage, ransack. It involves taking things illegally, and posits an act of the will.

QUICK QUIZ 24

Which one does not belong in this list?

(A) enervate   (B) sap   (C) invigorate   (D) devitalize

Pummel originally meant to beat someone with your fists. By extension, it means to take a beating by any means. It involves a violent attack, whether by man or by nature. In the context of a storm, a synonym would be pounded.

Q. So many people pronounce *especially* and *escape* as if they contain an "x," which they clearly do not. This drives me crazy, especially when the person saying it is well educated! Am I correct in believing that 'excape' and 'expecially' are not really words at all?

A. You are quite correct that even some educated people place that unnecessary -x- in those two words. But it's not a matter of intelligence. In many cases, it's a form of dyslexia. It even has a name: underdeveloped phonemic awareness. It shows up in other words, too: "sussess" for success, and "flustrated" for frustrated.

Paradoxically, these same people will usually spell the word correctly when writing it. The problem is with speech patterns.

Q. On your last show, I heard you say, "What we've got here . . . ." That should be, "What we have here . . ."

A. In formal writing or when giving a formal address, I agree with you. But in informal situations deliberately using a colloquial style, it is entirely proper.

Unlike many verbs, the verb "to get" has two spellings for its 3rd principal part: *have got* and *have gotten. The Columbia Guide to Standard American English* makes this distinction: "*I've got some money* means 'I have some money'; *I've gotten some money* means 'I've obtained some money.' As the contractions suggest, these locutions are primarily spoken."

I should add that *have got* is often used as a form of emphasis: "you have *got* to close your mouth when chewing." It would be less effective to say, "you have to close your mouth when chewing," although the idea would still be there.

Q. I'm curious about "get your goat."

A. I hope this doesn't provoke you to anger, but no one knows with certainty where "get your goat" comes from.

H.L. Mencken was a proponent of the race horse theory. The story went that skittish thoroughbreds were calmed by the presence of a pet goat in their stalls. If a rival owner stole the goat, the horse would be distraught, and the race would be in jeopardy. But there is no solid evidence that this practice was ever standard.

Life in Sing Sing, a book written in 1904, states that goat was prison slang for anger. But no one knows why the goat was chosen as a symbol. I know that they will attack if provoked, but so will a bull, a much more potent example of rage. So will many dogs, for that matter.

Q. When we get a real bargain, we say that we got it for a song. Why is that?

A. In Elizabethan times (Elizabeth I, that is), street performers were common. Singers would stand there and do their thing, and if spectators liked the sound, they might throw a penny or two. Singing was something that many people could do, it didn't take a great deal of effort, and it was met with meager rewards. So it became a symbol for something obtained at bargain prices.

Shakespeare wrote this in *All's Well That Ends Well*: "I know a man that had this tricke of melancholy hold a goodly Mannor for a song." [III. ii. 9]

Q. I have come across what seems to be an old-fashioned expression of disgust: *pshaw!* What can you tell me about this strange word?

A. It can express contempt, impatience, or disgust, or it can be used to depreciate or dismiss some statement or notion. Here's an example from *The Puritaine or the Widdow of Watling-streete[* 1607]: "Pshaw; a foolish Cozen of mine; I must thanke God for him." As for its origin, it

---

ANSWER 24   (B) INVIGORATE

Invigorate means to impart vitality.

Enervate, sap, and devitalize mean to drain vitality and energy.

---

may be a blending of shoo! (used to chase away chickens, 1483) and pah! (expressing disdain, 1592).

Q. While helping my daughter with her math homework last night, I noticed that one problem asked for a non-example. What the heck is that?

A. It's jargon that is now common in psychology or education. A non-example illustrates what is <u>not</u> being talked about. I would categorize the term as unnecessary and more than a little pretentious. Why not say a poor example, wrong example, inappropriate example, or just plain irrelevant example?

Trends like this seem to pop up like pimples every seven years or so. Old ideas are wrapped in a new package in an attempt to make them look fresh or compelling. When you reach behind the jargon to find substance, you often come up empty-handed.

Q. What is a kangaroo court?

A. There are a couple of definitions. First, it may be defined as an improperly constituted court with no legal standing whatsoever. This could occur during a prison riot when the inmates convict some of their own to death.

Second, it may be a properly constituted court that acts in an unfair, biased, and hasty way. In this sense, it goes back to the California Gold Rush. Many Australian immigrants were attracted by the promise of wealth, and they may have brought the image of a bounding kangaroo with them.

What's at question is who was doing the leaping, jumping, or hopping. One theory says that these courts were often convened to deal with claim jumpers; hence, the name. Another theory points to the system of itinerant judges in those days. They hopped from place to place, bringing organized justice with them. In some cases, they drew their salaries from the fines imposed on the guilty, so the unscrupulous and greedy amongst them may have jumped to convenient conclusions.

The term has entered official Supreme Court records. In Williams v. United States, Associate Justice William O. Douglas wrote, "Where police take matters in their own hands, seize victims, beat and pound them until they confess, there cannot be the slightest doubt that the police have deprived the victim of a right under the Constitution. It is the right of the accused to be tried by a legally constituted court, not by a kangaroo court."

Q.   My wife collects thimbles. What can you tell me about the linguistic side of the word?

A.   The word thimble is close in appearance to the word thumb, and that's no accident. Thimble tracks back to the Old English *thuma*, thumb. The *-le* ending sometimes signifies an instrument or tool, as in handle and paddle.
     Collectors of thimbles call themselves digitabulists, from the Latin *digitus*, a finger. [Pollicist, from the Latin word for thumb, might have been more appropriate.] A couple of other thumb words are pollical and pollicar, pertaining to the thumb.

Q.   Here's a headline from my local paper: "The upper class and the middle class are out of sink." I guess no one can accuse them of being all wet.

A.   That one should be spelled synch, of course, an abbreviation for synchronization. Here are a couple of other newspaper items spotted by readers:
     "A Traverse City man faces criminal charges after he allegedly tried to outrun police in his car." Must have been as big as a bus.
     "Four of the company's tow truck drivers answered about 40 calls for help between 2 and 10 a.m. Wednesday, each a 'wench out' from a drift or snow bank." OK now, no jokes about women drivers.

Q.   "Opportunity knocks"—where did that come from?

QUICK QUIZ 25

Which one does not belong in this list?

(A) bellicose   (B) irenic   (C) rancorous   (D) inimical

A.   I don't know the original source. Given more time, I might be able to track it down in a book of quotations, but I know that "opportunity knocks but once" is a favorite variation. American writer Louis L'Amour took exception to that: "Some say opportunity knocks only once. That is not true. Opportunity knocks all the time, but you have to be ready for it. If the chance comes, you must have the equipment to take advantage of it."

The word opportunity has a story buried deep within it. Literally, it means "towards Portunus." Portunus was the Roman god of harbors, and a ship about to enter a harbor was about to embrace shelter. Now it is any advantageous circumstance.

Q.   In retirement, I'm going back and rereading some of the classics. Right now, I'm working on Sir Walter Scott. One of his favorite words seems to be copse. At first, I though it was a misprint for corpse, but I see that it must be some kind of woods or grove of trees. Where did he get the word?

A.   Now that's my idea of retirement; you are a shining example for all of us. You're correct about the meaning. It refers to a thicket of trees. It is a corruption—or at least a modification—of the word coppice. It comes directly from the French, indirectly from a Latin word meaning to cut. The implication is that a copse was not simply decorative; it was a source of firewood.

Q.   I was watching a cable channel program about birth defects, and one of the words that they flashed on the screen was scaphocephaly. I took the time to write it down because I wanted to get back to you. From the show, I know that it is an abnormally long head, but I'm curious about the word itself.

A.   Literally, the word means "boat-shaped head." The- *cephal-* part comes from a Greek word meaning head, and the *-scaph-* portion comes from a Greek word meaning boat. Another word that uses it is scaphoid, a wrist bone found on the thumb side of the hand.

Q.   I'm a member of my church's Altar Society, and one of my duties is to arrange flowers for services. For Easter, we used gladiolas because they are showy and come in many colors. It occurred to me that the name is perfect: you feel glad and your heart lifts when you see them in profusion.

A.   I admire the etymology that you have placed on the flower, but the -glad- root doesn't mean happy. It comes from the Latin word for sword. The Latin writer Pliny, who wrote *A Natural History*, is credited with bestowing the name after noticing that the flower looked like an upraised sword.

Q.   I'm addicted to the Food Channel, and I especially enjoy Mario Batali, who spends a portion of his summer in this part of the world each year. Many of his meals include bruschetta, which is basically toast with a topping. I'm guessing that it contains the Italian word for brush, since you're supposed to brush on a mixture of olive oil and garlic as the first step. Am I right?

A.   This is a strange little word. The name comes from an Italian word that meant "to roast over coals." For toast, that makes sense. In turn, that came from a 13th century verb that meant "to pass a flame over the keel of a boat in order to melt the pitch and improve waterproofing." Ancient methods of waterproofing included bitumen, wax mixed with moss, and resin, so bringing a flame near the keel would melt the caulking material, thus spreading it more deeply into the cracks and joints.

Q.   Which is it, self-deprecating or self-depreciating?

A.   There are differences of opinion on this one. Sources such as the *Oxford English Dictionary* and Fowler's *Modern English Usage* take pains to show that deprecate originally meant "to avert by prayer," and

---

ANSWER 25   (B) IRENIC

Irenic means promoting peace.

Bellicose, rancorous, and inimical all promote animosity and hostility.

depreciate meant "to lessen in value," thus coming down on the side of self-depreciating.

But Bryan Garner (*Modern American Usage*) concludes, "However grudgingly, we must accord to [self-deprecating] the status of Standard English." And *Merriam-Webster's Concise Dictionary of English Usage* points out that self-deprecation is now the more common term, having supplanted the earlier self-depreciation. Thus, what started as a mistake has now been enshrined as an alternative.

Q.   Many cars that I see have a fish emblem on the trunk. Is there some kind of secret society in town?

A.   Nope, just a number of committed Christians. While the sign of the fish ultimately has pagan roots (it stood for feminine sexuality and the Great Mother), it was adopted as a symbol in the early church. The Greek word for fish would be transliterated as ichthus (*ixthus*), and this was turned into an acrostic.

Each letter represented a word: Iesus Xristos Theou 'Uios Soter, which translates as Jesus Christ, Son of God, Savior.

Fishing imagery was commonplace in the Bible. For instance, we find this in Matthew 4: 18-20: "And Jesus, walking by the sea of Galilee, saw two brethren, Simon called Peter, and Andrew his brother, casting a net into the sea: for they were fishers. And he saith unto them, 'Follow me, and I will make you fishers of men'. And they straightway left their nets, and followed him."

Q.   Is "your name is mud" connected with Dr. Samuel Mudd, the physician who treated John Wilke Booth's broken leg after Booth assassinated Abraham Lincoln?

A.   The thing to notice immediately is that the concept existed *before* Dr. Mudd was convicted of conspiracy. In other words, the saying did not arise from his predicament. Some would argue that his name intensified the cliché, but that's not something that can be proved. Mud is not Mudd.

Aside from its literal meaning, mud has been used figuratively since 1563 to represent something regarded as base, worthless, or polluting. It later developed the meaning of dregs—the lowest or worse part of something. By the 19th century, it also signified a dolt, an idiot. Jon Bee, nom de plume of author John Badcock, defined the epithet this way in his 1823 *Slang, A Dictionary of the Turf, the Ring, the Chase*: "Mud, a stupid twaddling fellow. 'And his name is mud!' ejaculated upon the conclusion of a silly oration, or of a leader in the Courier."

Today, if your name is mud, you are discredited and in disgrace. Your name has been dragged through the mire and you are the victim of merciless mudslingers. Dirty work, this.

Q. I hear quite a few people use *mano a mano* as if it meant man-to-man combat.

A. It is becoming quite popular, but it's still wrong. I heard political consultant Peter Fenn use it that way on CNN when he was speaking about an upcoming debate between Barack Obama and Hillary Clinton. Referring to the expected tussle, he said "It will be mano against . . .well . . . *not* mano." At least he didn't say womano.

Nay, nay, Mr. Fenn and a host of others. *Mano a mano* does not mean man to man, a mistake appearing far too frequently these days. Rather, it means hand to hand, and it comes to us from the Spanish, which borrowed it from the Latin *manus* (as in manual labor). Two women can fight *mano a mano*. This atrocity belongs in the Museum of the Misused, along with thinking that "begging the question" is the same as "raising the question" or "asking the question." It ain't.

Q. To beard the lion is a way of saying, to confront an opponent on his own territory. Why is that?

A. It's from the Old Testament: "And David said unto Saul, Thy servant kept his father's sheep, and there came a lion, and a bear, and took a lamb out of the flock. And I went out after him, and smote him, and delivered [it] out of his mouth; and when he arose against me, I caught [him] by his beard, and smote him, and slew him." [I Samuel 17:34-35]

Q. I'm taking a computer course, and I just learned that TCP/IP stands for Transmission Control Protocol/Internet Protocol. My question is, why protocol?

A. Protocol is used in a number of situations, but the common bond throughout is that it refers to established procedures (*"we've always done* *it that way"!*). In computer terminology, it's a set of rules for regulating the exchange of data between computers, and it includes the delightful image of a handshake. In international affairs, it could be called political etiquette. In business, it amounts to the company code of behavior. In historical use, it referred to an officially signed and verified transaction.

But it all began with the papyrus roll. Some of those rolls were attached to wooden rods or dowels, one at the beginning of the roll and the other at the end. In Greek, the word protocol broke into two parts: *proto*, first, and *kolla*, glue. The first part of the roll was glued to the left dowel, forming page one, as it were. That's where official identification and date would often appear.

The dowel at the far right side (the end of the roll) had a name, too: eschatocol. In Greek, the *eschat-* part meant last, and *-col*, as above, meant glue. Another fairly well-known word using the *eschat-* root is eschatology, the branch of theology that studies the end of the world.

Q.   Have you come across any more mondegreens?

A.   Mondegreens are misheard song lyrics, and as long as bands use amplifiers and singers scream, there will be plenty out there. Here are a few that listeners sent in.

Makin' carrot biscuits	Taking care of business [*Bachman Turner*]
She's got a tick in her eye	She's got a ticket to ride [*Beatles*]
If she had been paid for	If she had been faithful [*Chicago*]
Hit me with your pet shark	Hit me with your best shot [*Pat Benatar*]
Reverend blue jeans	Forever in blue jeans [*Neil Diamond*]
After the poison summer have gone	After the boys of summer have gone [*Don Henley*]
You make me eat, I'm gonna diet	You make me weak, I'm gonna die [*Journey*]

Q.   Steeplechase—where does that come from?

A.   Steeplechase horse racing, as opposed to flat racing, adds fences to the course for the horses to jump over.

A steeple is a lofty tower, usually connected to a church, and often containing the bells. It is built on the word steep, which denotes height and elevation.

The original steeplechase was an informal contest in which riders picked out a distant church tower and raced towards it. Whatever was in the way—hedges, bushes, ditches, fences—became part of the course.

Q.   A neighbor refers to his son as squirrelly. Is that an insult?

A.   At the very least, it means that your neighbor isn't pleased with the nervous and jumpy behavior exhibited by his child. It's based on a comparison to squirrels, who seldom travel in a straight line, and who stop and twitch their tails constantly.

   The word squirrel, by the way, contains a reference to their prominent feature, the bushy tail. In Greek, *skia* means shadow, and *ouros* means tail. Literally, the animal is a shadow tail.

Q.   I heard Dr. Gupta discussing jet lag, and one of the terms that he used was cicadian rhythm. Could you explain the word?

A.   A cicada is a noisy insect, something like a locust, so I'm fairly certain that the good doctor didn't say cicadian. Most likely, he said circadian rhythm. This is the 24-hour internal clock that affects the metabolism of most living creatures. It is formed from the Latin *circa*, approximately, and *dies*, day, so it's a rhythm spanning just about a day.

Q.   Where did "don't rock the boat" get started?

A.   It's much easier to say what it means. Most of us have ridden in canoes or rowboats with a rambunctious youngster or fidgety passenger, so we recognize it as a salutary warning not to mess with the equilibrium. It's pretty easy to upset the balance of a small craft, thus exposing oneself to the danger of tipping over.

   This is such a universal and ancient experience that I'd be surprised if someone were able to cite the very first literal use of the term. Metaphorically, it means to let things be, to avoid upsetting routine ways, to honor the status quo. It is akin to another nautical warning, *don't make waves.*

   The idiom seems to reflect a cautious streak in human behavior, so I suppose we could pair it with *don't change horses at midstream,*

QUICK QUIZ 26

Which one does not belong in this list?

(A) instigate   (B) quash   (C) extirpate   (D) quell

along with *let sleeping dogs lie.* Tie them all together and we have *don't rock the dog to sleep at midstream.* Sound advice, dawg.

Q.	I overheard someone say that she was on tender hooks while waiting to see if her bid on a house was going to be accepted, but I'm not really sure what she meant. Any help?

A.	First of all, if you looked for that phrase, you probably found nothing. What she said (or *should* have said) was that she was on tenterhooks. It's easy to mishear D's and T's because they are formed in the same area of the mouth, with the tongue touching the teeth.

This takes us back to 15th century cloth makers. When cloth was milled and dyed, it was stretched on a wooden framework so that it would not shrink or lose shape as it dried. The wooden frame was called a tenter, perhaps deriving from the Latin *tendere,* to stretch.

The tenter-hooks were the close-set hooks or nails set into the wooden framework to hold the cloth; they suspended the cloth in a uniform fashion. Eventually, tenterhooks acquired the figurative meaning of something causing painful suspense.

The cliché *to be on tenterhooks* was set in place by British novelist Tobias Smollett in his hilarious *Roderick Random* [1748]: "I left him upon the tenter-hooks of impatient uncertainty."

Q.	As I was listening to my favorite oldies station today, I heard Ray Charles singing *Smack Dab in the Middle,* and I said to myself, I have to ask the Professor about that one.

A.	In essence, the phrase means "slapped precisely in the center." According to the *Oxford English Dictionary,* **smack-dab** showed up in print in 1892: "He hit him smack dab in the mouth" [*Dialect Notes* I, 232].

The first element, **smack,** is used as an adverb. It is defined as "with, or as with, a smack; suddenly and violently; slap." It appears in 1782 in Cowper's *John Gilpin:* "Smack went the whip, round went the wheels."

The second element, **dab,** means "with a dab or sudden contact." Robert Armin's *Nest of Ninnies* uses it in this sense in 1608: "He dropt downe..as heauy as if a leaden plummet... had fallen on the earth dab."

A variation is **slap-dab**. **Slap-bang** is close, but it meant immediately rather than centered: "Slap-bang shop: a petty cook's shop where there is no credit given, but what is had must be paid down with the ready slap-bang, i.e. immediately" [1785, Grose's *Dictionary of the Vulgar Tongue*].

Q.   While doing some research for class, I came across an article from 1927 titled, *Botanical Gleanings in Michigan*. What's the import of the word gleanings?

A.   Used as a metaphorical term, **gleaning** refers to gathering odds and ends of information bit by bit and placing them in one written piece. The word *gleanings* shows up in the title of many books and pamphlets, a surprising number of them about local history or about religious meditations. The word tracks back to a verb found both in Old French (*glener*) and Late Latin (*glenare*).

To glean was to wander through fields that had already been harvested in order to gather the scraps left behind by the reapers. The most famous gleaner was Ruth, who benefited from the generosity of Boaz. [Ruth 2: 1-14]

Not only was leaving material for the poor to glean an act of kindness, it was seen as a religious obligation: "And when ye reap the harvest of your land, thou shalt not wholly reap the corner of thy field, neither shalt thou gather the gleaning of thy harvest. And thou shalt not glean thy vineyard, neither shalt thou gather the fallen fruit of thy vineyard; thou shalt leave them for the poor and for the stranger: I am the Lord your God." [Leviticus 19:9–10]

Q.   What can you tell me about the word trinket?

A.   First, its origin is uncertain. The *Oxford English Dictionary* suggests there is a slender chance that it may be related to the phrase

---

ANSWER 26   (A) INSTIGATE

Instigate means to start something.

Quash, extirpate, and quell mean to stop something.

"to trick out," meaning to decorate with baubles or trifling ornaments. That fits its usual meaning, a small ornament or fancy article, usually an article of jewelry for personal adornment.

Trinket and *trinketing* in the sense "items of little value" are enjoying a revival thanks to computer games. Trinketing means the mage used his trinkets to become much more powerful for a few seconds in order to win the fight.

Q.   This just doesn't sound right: "The Michigan House and Senate must nip the budget crisis in the butt, not pass a temporary measure that only defers the problem."

A.   I used to have a feisty Westie named McDuff. My brother used to tease the dog when McDuff was a puppy, so there was no love lost. In fact, we used to encourage McDuff's frequent nipping attacks, everyone hollering, "Bite him on the butt!"

I bring this up only because it gives some insight into why someone might hear *nip it in the bud* and think that it alluded to a terrier snapping at someone's glutes. The essential problem is that it then refers to action: an attack on the part of the animal and a retreat on the part of the victim.

In contrast, *Nip it in the bud* actually means to stop something before it becomes serious or significant. It was originally a gardening term, and it refers to removing or severing a bud by pinching or snipping it off. Too many buds on the same stalk lead to inferior flowers or plants, so this is a form of botanical birth control.

Q.   Here's a headline from a New York newspaper: "Handsome cab horse killed in Central Park accident"

A.   This falls into the category known as eggcorns—incorrect substitutions that result from words not clearly heard or mistaken for others. [See *The Eggcorn Database* at http://eggcorns.lascribe.net/]

It actually should have read Hansom cab. Joseph Hansom of Leicestershire, England, patented a vehicle with some of the earlier features of this type of cab. A Hansom cab was a low-hung two-wheeled cabriolet holding two persons inside, the driver on an elevated seat behind, and the reins running over the roof. It had a low center of gravity for safety in cornering.

133

The newspaper story went on to give some details of the accident: A Central Park carriage horse was killed Friday afternoon in what is being described as a "freak accident" along Central Park South. Police say it started when a 12-year-old mare named "Smoothie" was spooked by someone playing a snare drum after four o' clock Friday afternoon. The horse then ran into the street with the carriage still attached and struck a tree.

"Nobody should be allowed to set up a snare drum set or any kind of drum set without a parade permit right near to the horse's ears," said a witness.

So if you wish to beat your drum in Central Park, you had better hold a document near the horse's head.

Q. I have been wondering about the origin of the word nightmare. My mother used to compare it to a frightened rider clinging for dear life to a runaway horse, unable to make the animal turn or slow down. Is that where the word came from?

A. This is another case of history eventually producing two words with identical spellings, but coming from totally different sources. When you look up the -*mare* segment, you find mare^{-1} and mare^{-2}.

Mare^{-1} comes from an Old English word meaning horse. Mare^{-2} comes from various Germanic cognates meaning a malevolent female spirit. Nightmare is built on the latter root. The nightmare would pounce upon the sleeping person's chest, thus producing a feeling of suffocation. This would lead to distress and fright, the hallmarks of a nightmare.

Medieval stories are filled with night-visiting demons who had sexual intercourse with their victims in order to perpetuate the demon race. The incubus was male, while the succubus was female.

Q. My teacher takes points off when we use an exclamation point. I don't think that's fair!

QUICK QUIZ 27

Which one does not belong in this list?

(A) specious   (B) sophistical   (C) fallacious   (D) veritable

A.   Exclamation points are like simulated orgasms; they display intense feelings where none may actually exist. They attempt to spur us into a frenzy while watching dispassionately from the corner of their beady little eyes. If you were never again to use an exclamation point, your writing would not suffer.

They show up with great frequency in forwarded emails, especially the ones that purport to save us from some imminent danger. My recommendation is that when you receive an email sagging from the weight of color highlighting, screaming uppercase letters, impudent boldface, and scary exclamation points, you should head straight for the delete key.

WE'VE GOT TO STOP THIS INSANITY!!!!!!!!!!!!!!!!!!!!!!!!!!!!

Q.   Knols seems to be the new computer buzzword. What do you know about it?

A.   Only what I've read in *Wired Magazine*. The word stands for units of knowledge, and it represents a forthcoming attempt by Google to increase the human element in searches. Human authors, rather than trolling software, will compile authoritative "must-read" articles that will be placed prominently high in search results.

You might want to check this site for ongoing developments: http://www.writegreatknols.com/

Q.   The word monopoly confuses me because it contains elements that seem to cancel each other out: *mono-*, one, and *-poly*, many.

A.   I admire your thoughfulness. What is throwing you is the second element. It comes from the Greek word *polein*, to sell, not from *poly*. It shows up in words such as bibliopoly (bookselling), duopoly (domination of a market by two companies), oligopoly (a market controlled by a few companies), pharmacopoly (drugstore), and, of course, our starting point, monopoly (domination of a market by one company).

Q.   Is there really a hand in handsome? If so, how?

A.   Let's examine the *-some* part first. It was an Old English suffix

(-*sum*) used primarily to form adjectives from nouns, and occasionally from other adjectives and verbs.

So the suffix -*some* added to *hand* meant "pertaining to a hand." Let's follow the evolution of the word, starting in 1435 A.D., through the eyes of the *Oxford English Dictionary.*

- Easy to handle or manipulate, or to wield, deal with, or use in any way.
- Of action, speech, etc.: Appropriate, apt, dexterous, clever, happy: in reference to language, sometimes implying gracefulness of style.
- Proper, fitting, seemly, becoming, decent, courteous, gracious.
- Of a sum of money, a fortune, a gift, etc.: Considerable. Now in stronger sense: Ample, generous, liberal, munificent.
- Having a fine form or figure (usually in conjunction with full size or stateliness); 'beautiful with dignity'; 'fine'. (The prevailing current sense.)

So, "attractive because easy to handle" eventually lost the hand but retained the attractiveness.

Q. A commentator covering the Master's Golf Tournament said, "You can hear the wind whisking through the pines." That can't possibly be right, can it?

A. Another eggcorn, I'd say. Whisk means to move with a light stroking motion, to sweep using a brush, and to stir or beat up food with a light rapid movement.

Your commentator was reaching for a cliché, but he blew right past it: *the wind whistling through the pines.*

Q. What will headline writers do without Limbo?

ANSWER 27   (D) VERITABLE

Veritable means true.

Specious, sophistical, and fallacious mean false.

A. Good question. Limbo refers to the permanent place or state of those unbaptized children who, even though they committed no personal mortal sin, are excluded from the presence of God after death because of original sin. They were not damned and they lived in a state of happiness, but they were not in the direct presence of God, which is the essence of heaven.

But in the spring of 2007, Pope Benedict XVI virtually repealed Limbo, saying that there is hope that these infants do enjoy the Beatific Vision after all. Last one out turn off the lights.

In Latin, *limbus* meant a hem or a fringe. Limbo was the ablative singular form, translated as *on the fringe*. So Limbo was a suburb between hell and heaven, so near yet so far.

By extension, it came to mean a place of confinement, sort of a junkyard for the outworn or useless. To be in limbo is to be out of the mainstream, on permanent hold, up in the air.

Selected headlines make it clear that it is a very popular metaphor:

- Court leaves status of Miss. executions in limbo [MSNBC, August 8, 2007]
- Case in limbo against bounty hunter [USA Today, July 27, 2007]
- Culpepper signs with Raiders; Russell still in limbo [ESPN, August 1, 2007]
- Transplant patients in limbo as doctors quit [ABC News, August 6, 2007]
- Budget standoff: Budget vote left senator in limbo [Sacramento Bee, August 3, 2007]

Q. Allow me to share a gaffe that showed up in a photo caption. The photo showed Bob Nardelli in a sexy-looking Chrysler, and the caption read, "Chrysler's boss shows his metal at car rally."

A. My first reaction also was that he should have written mettle. Mettle is a person's strength of character, disposition, courage, and temperament. The cliché is *to show one's mettle*, and it means to reveal your inner self during adversity. Then it dawned on me that the writer was perpetrating a pun. In the story, Bob Nardelli is showing off his car — a hunk of metal.

But it turns out that metal and mettle are related in history. In Anglo-Norman, metal took on the meaning of material or substance. It was then applied metaphorically to a person's substance or nature. In fact, the spelling metal was used both for the malleable stuff and for the Right Stuff.

The OED points out the interchangeability in two versions of Shakespeare's 1 Henry IV, II.v.

- 1598 Quarto Edition: "A Corinthian, a lad of metall."
- 1623 Folio Edition: "A Corinthian, a lad of mettle."

Don't meddle with a lad with mettle; he deserves a metal medal.

Q. "I'm curious about the word bayonet. I can see the word 'bay' buried in there, along with 'net,' but I can't see how those words would relate to a stabbing weapon attached to the barrel of a rifle."

A. The *Oxford English Dictionary* casts some doubt, but the usual explanation is that the instrument was either invented or first used in the city of Bayonne, France, in the 16th century.

Words often do arise from a place name with which an object is associated.

- The artesian well was developed in Artois, a province in France.
- A cantering horse moves at a moderate gallop, and it derives from Canterbury, England, where pilgrims on horseback visited the shrine of Thomas à Becket.
- Bubbly champagne properly comes only from Champagne, a region in northeast France.
- The ermine, whose fur is prized for decoration, probably took its name from the country of Armenia.
- A laconic person—a person of few words—owes his name to the tight-lipped inhabitants of Laconia in southern Greece.
- To meander means to wander, and its name comes from the Meander River in Phrygia, noted for its twists and turns.
- Sodomy comes from the biblical city of Sodom, destroyed by God along with Gomorrah because of industrial-strength vice and depravity. [See Genesis 19]

Q.   Someone who is curt is rude. Does that mean you shouldn't name your baby Curt?

A.   There are those who claim that our names determine our destiny, but in this case, curt comes from the Latin *curtus*, short. I doubt that the name would stunt a child's growth.

Curtus meant short, deficient in height, but there were intimations of mutilation and breakage lurking beneath the surface. It was a word that might be applied to a castrated bull, a gelded horse, a dog with a docked tail, or a circumcised man. [Gentlemen in the audience may now participate in a group wince.]

By the time this root worked its way into English, it had acquired the meaning of physically short or abbreviated, though the cutting aspect had not entirely disappeared. So we had the following:

* curtal (an animal with a short tail)
* curtate (shortened or abbreviated)
* curtail (to shorten)
* curtilage (a small enclosure)
* curtipendulous (hanging by a short stem)
* decurtate (shortened)

By extension, the English word curt left the realm of the merely physical and came to mean terse to an extreme degree—bordering, in fact, on rudeness, as you pointed out.

Q.   What can you tell me about the word debauch?

A.   We debauch people when we corrupt their morals or principles. We lead them astray from their duties or proper allegiances. Often, impurity or unchaste actions are involved. Ethical erosion is at the heart of the matter.

That's why it's interesting to learn that the word arose from carpenters and masons chipping away at building materials.

The carpenter would rough-hew a timber, as opposed to building fine furniture with perfectly smooth surfaces. In other words, he would hack away at the timber just enough to produce a relatively flat surface; you could still see the adze marks when he was finished. Such timbers often acted as roof supports, and to this day, that rough-hewn aspect is a prized feature. In Germanic, bauch at one time meant a beam.

In the case of the stonemason, he would hack away at a row or course of stones in order to make them serviceably flat. At one point in history, a bauche was a hut built of stones. So, just as a builder would change materials from their original, pristine state, so would the debaucher hack away at the soul of the innocent.

Q.   Why are <u>all</u> sports enthusiasts called fans? It's only baseball that uses *fan* to signify a strikeout.

A.   Fan in this case is an abbreviation of fanatic. Fanatic comes to us from the Latin word *fanum*, a temple. Avid devotees of a particular god would invite possession, whereby the favored god would induce a frenzy. The person would be figuratively carried away, exhibiting behavior akin to madness.

Enthusiasm, a quality displayed in fans, originally meant possessed by a god. The *theos* (god) was *ev*, within.

Frantic and frenzy are two words that would suit such an occasion, and they are related. Frantic comes from a Greek form meaning affected with delirium (*phrenetikos*). Frenzy comes from the same basic Greek root.

Phren was a Greek word meaning mind, and it has given us phrenesis (madness), phrenetic (mentally deranged), phreniatric (relating to mental disorder), phrenitic (delirious), and others.

Nowadays, frenzy is no longer seen as a gift of the gods.

Q.   I saw a headline the other day that read, *Sox Pummel Tigers*. I know that sportswriters love alliteration and hate to use plain words like *defeat*, but isn't this stretching things?

A.   You're correct that it means to beat, and I love your comment about sportswriters, but it's a legitimate word. As just one example, Charles Dickens used it in *Great Expectations*: "Then, he and my sister would pair off in such nonsensical speculations about Miss Havisham, and about what she would do with me and for me, that I used to want - quite painfully - to burst into spiteful tears, fly at Pumblechook, and **pummel**

QUICK QUIZ 28

Which one does not belong in this list?

(A) attenuated   (B) meager   (C) capacious   (D) sparse

him all over." So, as a verb it means to beat someone, especially with the fists.

Brewer's *Dictionary of Phrase and Fable* gives it a French origin—pommeler, to dapple—because it's a matter of beating someone black and blue. The OED sees a connection to a word meaning an ornamental knob.

The noun pummel (also spelled pommel) covers a wide range of objects, but they all have something in common: a bulbous appearance. Here are some of its meanings.

- the ornamental knob on a candlestick
- a finial
- the ornamental top of a flagpole
- the knob at the back end of a cannon
- a cross with knobs at the end of the arms
- the knob at the end of a sword or dagger that keeps it from slipping out of your grasp
- the knob on a saddle used for mounting and dismounting
- a woman's breast
- the lower side of a closed fist
- in gymnastics, the curved handgrip on a vaulting horse

Q. A frequent cliché is "fraught with danger." What can you tell me about the word fraught?

A. You're correct: fraught is usually followed by ominous phrases such as "with danger," "with peril," or "with risk." As it turns out, its close relative is the word freight.

Originally, fraught stood for the money paid for a transport vessel or the act of transport itself. Later, the noun designated the cargo in the hold. It ended as any burden or load. In Sir James Barrie's *Little Minister*, we find the line ". . . to carry a fraught of water to the manse." According to the OED, this would have amounted to two pailfuls.

At various times, the verb form meant to load a ship, to hire a vessel, and to equip. The past participle (fraught) means (1) attended with, (2) carrying something with it as an attribute or accompaniment, or (3) filled with promise or menace.

Q. A smooth-talking sales person is said to be using patter. Is that because he gets you all excited, making the heart beat faster?

A. You mean as in pitter-patter? No, in the colloquial sense, patter is defined as mere talk or incessant chatter. In sales or entertainment, it is the smooth, persuasive, and sometimes rapid speech used to attract an audience and then keep its attention.

Patter came from the rapid and mechanical way in which the *Pater noster* (the *Our Father*) was often repeated, e.g. in the rosary. The words would tumble out automatically with no thought given to meaning. Of course, the automatic nature of the prayers used in the rosary was supposed to give the reciter an opportunity to meditate on theological mysteries, so it wasn't just an act of sloppiness.

[Pater noster, qui es in caelis: / Our Father, who art in heaven:]

Q. I'm writing a novel (or trying, anyway), and I notice that I'm using "he said" and "she said" too frequently. Can you suggest a really good thesaurus that will supply me with dialogue verbs?

A. Don't be too quick to jettison a useful verb. In the past, *The New Yorker* had one of the best editorial staffs in the business. "One of the rules, according to James Thurber, was that a passage of dialogue is best followed by *said*. Anything else—*shouts* or *exclaims* or *retorts*, for example—is just wasted motion. No verb, in other words, should substitute for said." [from *"Shut Up!" He Explained*, by William Noble, Paul S. Erickson, Publisher, 1987, p.91]

That's a bit extreme, perhaps, but it errs on the side of the angels. It's a rule that more writers should observe, especially in stories posted on the internet. I did a quick and dirty search and found groaners such as these:

- "I wonder if the wishbone she gave me would have done any good," cried Cecily suddenly.
- "I'll probably continue to smoke," he averred.

ANSWER 28   (C) CAPACIOUS

Capacious means spacious and roomy.
Attenuated, meager, and sparse signify deficiency.

- "I'll never forgive myself for not thinking about it before," mourned Cecily.
- "Oh, let's go to bed," growled Dan.
- "You might tell me all about it, Sara," I insinuated.
- You've got to give the spell time to work," he expostulated.
- "Sorry," she demurred. "I scratched necrophilia off my list a long time ago."
- "And that's their right," he opined.

The New Yorker policy now allows substitutions for *said*, but Noble points out that leaving out any modifier at all—even *he/she said*—allows the dialogue to speak for itself. Omission is a good way to change the rhythm and pace and avoid needless repetition. But never undervalue the word *said*. Straining for synonyms is counterproductive, he pontificated.

Q. I saw an ad describing a cell phone (Casio) as sturdy. This just doesn't strike me as appropriate. Oak furniture is sturdy. A cast-iron stove is sturdy. A front-end loader is sturdy.

A. I see your point. Sturdy is a plain, blue-collar type of word. It evokes images of vigor, robustness, hardiness, strength, and solidity.

That's why it's surprising to learn that in its long history, it has also meant giddy, dazed, reckless, ruthless, cruel, rebellious, obstinate, and surly. It was also the name of a brain disease in sheep and cattle.

Even stranger is the putative origin of the word, though no one seems to be absolutely certain. Some authorities say that it comes from the Latin word meaning thrush: *turdus*. This is because in the early days of its existence, it meant thoughtless or feather-brained. It reflected a French proverb, "drunk as a thrush." The idea was that if a bird eats fermented fruit, it will act drunk; giddiness and recklessness will follow.

"The only birds I see are a few sad survivors of a covey of partridges and thrushes, which conduct themselves so strangely that the foresters assert that they are tipsy. 'As drunk as a thrush' is a proverb here." [Charles Dickens, *Household Words: A Weekly Journal*, p. 308]

Q. I maintain that the *barrow* in wheelbarrow is actually a corruption of burro, the pack animal. After all, both are used to transport materials. Over the course of centuries, the word burro was misheard, misspelled, and otherwise mangled until the transformation was complete.

A.   Brilliant folk etymology. If enough people pick up on this, it will soon begin appearing in endlessly forwarded emails.

Unfortunately, the *Oxford English Dictionary* will have none of this. Instead, it soberly reminds us that barrow comes from an Old English word meaning "to bear or to carry," and it showed up in print as *barewe* in the year 1300. The earliest model was a framework with handles projecting fore and aft so that two men could carry things. To distinguish it from a wheelbarrow, it was called a hand-barrow.

The spelling *barrow* was also used for several wildly unrelated items:

- a mountain or a hill
- a gravemound formed from dirt or stones
- a castrated boar
- a conical basket into which wet salt is placed to drain
- a long sleeveless flannel garment for infants

Of course, those in the know realize that the original spelling was wheelborrow, and that it targeted the practice of neighbors who use your yard equipment, then forget to return it.

Q.   I was at my doctor's office last week, and the nurse who did the screening told me at one point that she was looking for crepitation. I was too embarrassed to ask what that meant.

A.   If she was checking your respiration at that point, she was looking for a dry, crackling sound in the lungs. *The American Heritage Medical Dictionary* also defines it as "the sensation felt on placing the hand over the seat of a fracture when the broken ends of the bone are moved, or over tissue in which gas gangrene is present."

The word comes from the Latin, where *crepitare* meant to crackle. Decrepit means worn out from old age, illness, or hard use, and decrepitude is the noun signifying that state or condition. Figuratively, things have cracked open. To decrepitate is to subject crystals or salts to

---

QUICK QUIZ 29

Which one does not belong in this list?

(A) discernment   (B) sagacity   (C) imprudence   (D) discrimination

high heat so that they crackle and disintegrate. Finally, a crepitaculum is the name herpetologists use for the rattler of the rattlesnake.

Q.   Traditionally, schools play Elgar's *Pomp and Circumstance* as a processional in graduation ceremonies. Can you explain the title?

A.   If Elgar's descendents get royalties each time the piece is played, they must be millionaires. He wrote the suite for the coronation of King Edward VII.

Pomp comes from a Greek word meaning procession, parade, or display. In Latin, *circumstantia* signified a surrounding condition, and one of the meanings acquired in English was a ceremony or a formal presentation. So, *Procession and Ceremony* would be synonymous.

The pairing was forever established by William Shakespeare in his *Othello*, Act III, Scene iii:

> Oh now, for euer
> Farewell the Tranquill minde; farewell Content;
> Farewell the plumed Troopes, and the bigge Warres,
> That makes Ambition, Vertue! Oh farewell,
> Farewell the neighing Steed, and the shrill Trumpe,
> The Spirit-stirring Drum, th' Eare-piercing Fife,
> The Royall Banner, and all Qualitie,
> Pride, Pompe, and Circumstance of glorious Warre:
> And O you mortall Engines, whose rude throates
> Th' immortall Ioues dread Clamours, counterfet,
> Farewell: Othello's Occupation's gone.

Q.   I came across the word propinquity in my Sociology textbook. It just seems to be a $10 word for closeness. Is it legitimate?

A.   If by that you mean, is it a real word, the answer is yes. If you mean, should we endorse bloated language, the answer is no. I'm assuming that you're reading about what sociologists call *The Propinquity Effect*. Harburg and Lane, who wrote *Finian's Rainbow*, put it succinctly: "When I'm not near the girl I love, I love the girl I'm near."

It comes from the Latin *propinquus*, near or neighboring, and it means a closeness or proximity. It has also been used to signify a nearness in time, not just distance. In addition, it can refer to kinship or to similar dispositions or belief.

Variations include propinquant (adjacent), propinquate (proximate), propinquous (close at hand), and the obsolete propinque (immediate, proximate).

I was surprised and delighted to discover a rare antonym: longinquity, remoteness in space or in time. I think that's a word that deserves to be revived. It is related to the also rare longinque (distant).

Q. Why do we say, for crying out loud?

A. I think that we're looking at another minced oath here. If you recall, a minced oath (also generically called a euphemism) is a disguised way of saying something considered sacred and therefore not to be used in casual or profane conversation.

We see it in phrases such as Jeepers Creepers (*Jesus Christ!*), Holy Moly (*holy mother of God!*), Great Scott (*Great God!*), cripes (*Christ!*) and dozens of others.

In this case, it's a teaser. When you hear the opening syllables (for cry. . .), you expect to hear "for Christ's sake"! as the completion. "For crying out loud" thus titillates, but it doesn't directly offend.

As a side note, we usually associate the word mince with cutting or grinding up meat (as in mincemeat pie), but it evolved into "deprived of an essential part or abbreviated" by the 17th century.

Q. I found this in a history book: "A gremial was a permanent resident in the University." Maybe it's just my quirky mind, but the first thing I thought of was a gremlin.

A. Gremlin is a fairly recent coinage. It seems to have arisen in the R.A.F. during WWII as an explanation for glitches in aircraft. Gremial is a *much* older word.

In Latin, gremium meant the lap or bosom, and that provided us with this strange, but useful, term.

ANSWER 29   (C) IMPRUDENCE

Imprudence relates to poor judgment.

Discernment, sagacity, and discrimination relate to sound judgment.

Gremial refers to a tight membership. The word started in academic circles, where it referred to a resident member of a university. That was appropriate, since the university was the Alma Mater (fostering mother).

Later, it was extended to any society or corporation, where it referred to full members, as opposed to honorary members. It was also applied to any bosom-buddy, any intimate friend.

Finally, gremial came to mean an ecclesiastical garment, an apron placed on a bishop's lap when he was seated. Its purpose was to keep his costly vestments from being stained. The cleaning bills were ungodly.

Q. During an interview on CNBC this week, the host referred to a guest as a "stock market maven." Where did that word come from?

A. Maven comes to us courtesy of the Yiddish *meyvn* (plural *mevinim*) an expert or connoisseur. That is a variation of the Hebrew *mebin*, a person with understanding, a teacher. The word is the participial form of *hebin*, to understand, to attend to, to teach.

The word was around in the 1950s, but it received wider notoriety because of an advertising campaign for Vita Herring, launched in the United States in 1964.The ads featured a character known as "The Beloved Herring Maven."

Other names for experts or connoisseurs include enthusiast, aficionado, ace, adept, authority, genius, hotshot, master, pundit, sensation, star, virtuoso, whizkid, and wizard.

Media are also fond of the word *guru*. Guru is a Hindu term for a teacher or priest. In Sanskrit, the word meant weighty, grave, and dignified. Originally signifying the head of a religious sect, it was eventually secularized into an expert or teacher in more worldly arts.

Q. Where did the word budget come from?

A. The word budget comes from the French *bouge*, a bag, usually made of leather. A bougette was a small bag or wallet.

Thick leather sacks of various sizes were used by workmen to carry nails and tools. Sharp points or edges would have penetrated other materials, so it was a matter of safe transport.

The name was soon applied to a small purse or wallet used to store money. As long as there was something left in the little leather purse, you were within budget.

Wyclif's Bible contained the base word *bouge* in Psalm 32:7, though in an image that seems a bit strained to contemporary ears: "And he gaderith togidere the watris of the see as in a bowge; and settith depe watris in tresours." [And he gathers together the waters of the sea as in a leather pouch.]

Q. I saw a bumper sticker yesterday advertising *Scab Skateboard.* How appropriate for someone who skins elbows and knees!

A. Most of us think of scab as the crusty protection that forms over a scrape or wound—nature's own bandage. But the word started its career in 1250 as the name for a disease of the skin in which pustules or scales are formed. Take my word for it: the medical illustrations are disgusting.

It was also a disease in animals resembling mange, a condition characterized by itching, lesions, and loss of hair. [Mange comes from a word meaning *to eat.* In Latin, it was not unusual for the same word to mean itching and eating, probably from the analogy that an itch gnaws away at your skin.] Not to be limited in its scope, the word scab was also applied to plant diseases. It caused scab-like roughness on vegetable surfaces.

The word was also used as an epithet referring to a scoundral or scurrilous person. And, of course, in labor history it was applied to someone who refused to join a strike or who took the place of a striking worker.

Around 1529, it took on theological dimensions, being used to describe a moral or spiritual disease. A great quote in this regard comes from one G. Herbert: "The itch of disputing is the scab of the church." Amen to that, brother.

Scabies is an allied word, as are scabious, scabrate, scabridity, scabriusculous, scabrosity, scabrous, and the highly picturesque scabland,

---

Quick Quiz 30

Which one does not belong in this list?

(A) furtive (B) overt (C) surreptitious (D) clandestine

an elevated area of barren rocky land with little or no soil cover, deeply scarred by channels of ancient glacial streams.

Scabbard—a sheath that protects the blade of a sword or knife—is not connected.

Q. What does caveat emptor mean? It appeared in a recent edition of *Consumer Reports.*

A. It means let the buyer beware, and it is Latin. The -empt- root worked its way into English, but most of these words are now obsolete:

- coemption: The buying up of the whole supply of any commodity in the market.
- emption: The action of buying: chiefly in phrases, *right of (sole) emption*, etc.
- emptional: That may be purchased
- emptitious: Venal, capable of being bought.
- emptor: A purchaser.
- emptory: A mart, market-place.

I propose reviving the word *emptorial*, defined as "of or pertaining to buying." Thus, we would have emptorial frenzy, emptorial sprees, emptorial considerations and concerns, emptorial opportunities, emptorial compulsion, and emptorial trends or patterns.

The word is not a total invention. The word actually appeared in the 1922 edition of *Roget's International Thesaurus*, edited by Mawson. In that edition, it appeared under 795: Purchase.

Q. Today's edition of [a local newspaper] contained this sentence in an article in the Sports Section: "Quite a story for a guy who's first swimming lesson was 10 years ago." Shouldn't that be *whose*?

A. It most definitely should. Good call on your part. The easiest solution is to remember that *who's* is a contraction. It stands for *who is*; the apostrophe replaces the -i-. Saying "a guy who is first swimming lesson . . ." out loud should tip you off to the error. Correct examples would include

- Who's your daddy?
- I asked him who's in charge.

149

- Who's responsible for this mess?

If you've never heard the "Who's on First" routine of Abbott and Costello, read it here: http://www.baseball-almanac.com/humor4.shtml

Whose is a possessive pronoun, and it may be rendered as *belonging to whom*. It always involves ownership or intimate connection. Here are some correct uses:

- This is a word whose origins are lost in the mists of history.
- When I find out whose wallet this is, I'll return it.
- Quite a story for a guy whose first swimming lesson was 10 years ago.

A famous use of the word may be found in the opening lines of Robert Frost's *Stopping by Woods on a Snowy Evening*.

Q. I recently read a book about Governor Granholm of Michigan. The author wrote, "I followed the governor with cameraman in toe." That would require either a gigantic foot or a shrunken cameraman.

A. The image required is of being "in tow," pulled by a line by another vessel. In Old English, it could refer to anything being hauled or dragged, but by the 14th century, it was applied almost exclusively to ships.

"In tow" is matched by another error involving a homonym. I have come across "tow the line," meaning to abide by the rules and regulations. I can see where pulling a barge attached to a hawser might spring to mind, but in this case it should be "toe the line."

Many of the early uses of this image come from the British Navy, so many commentators think that it started with sailors in formation. The space between deck planks was filled with loose hemp or jute fiber (oakum), then sealed with pitch. As a result, dark lines ran the length of the deck. When the crew was required to fall into formation for inspection or instruction, they would place the toes of their boots on a designated line to achieve a neat formation. American sailors favored the phrase, "toe the crack."

Q. I used to hear the word flibbertigibbet more in the past than I do now. Where did it come from? We used it to mean a flighty person.

A.   According to the *Oxford English Dictionary*, it is onomatopoeia (where the sound of the word suggests its meaning). In its early form, it was spelled flybbergybe, and it meant a chattering or gossiping person. (An obsolete meaning of gibbet was to whoop or cry out to signal to your dog that the hunt was on.)

By Shakespeare's time, it was one of the names that signified a minor devil or demon. He seems to have read a book by Samuel Harsnet with the delightful title, *Declaration of Egregious Popish Impostures.* A few of the names mentioned in Harsnet show up in King Lear, including our focus today:

Edgar This is the foul fiend Flibbertigibbet: he begins at curfew, and walks till the first cock; he gives the web and the pin, squints the eye, and makes the harelip; mildews the white wheat, and hurts the poor creature of earth.   [*Lear* III. iv.]

In the works of Scott, Coleridge, and Stevenson, it lost some of the diabolocal baggage and referred to someone mischievous or flighty.

If you have seen *Sound of Music*, you know that it was used in a song:

> How do you solve a problem like Maria?
> How do you catch a cloud and pin it down?
> How do you find a word that means Maria?
> A flibbertijibbet! A will-o'-the wisp! A clown!

That has probably extended its life.

Q.   Where did the word tragedy come from?

A.   There is no question that it came from ancient Greek rites that eventually developed into theater, and it is usually said to mean "goat song." Speculation abounds as to why goats were involved.

One theory says that in song contests, the prize was a goat, or that goats were sacrificed as offerings.

Another theory points to performances during religious ceremonies honoring Dionysus. Legend has it that they involved satyrs, creatures who were half goat and half human.

Then there are those who say that the *-trag-* root came not from the word goat, but from the verb *to gnaw*. Eat your heart out.

Another -trag- term never made it into English as far as I know, but the Greeks had a word that would be rendered as *tragomaskhalos* in English. It meant "with armpits smelling like a he-goat." Better head for the industrial-strength deodorant section, Billy.

Q.   An article I'm reading about medieval cathedrals refers to gargoyles and grotesques. Gargoyles I've heard of.

A.   The distinction that art historians seem to make is that gargoyles were actually waterspouts in disguise. They received their name from the French *gargouille*, throat. Other carved figures that are not waterspouts should be called grotesques.

The -esque suffix means *resembling* or *in the manner of*, so grotesque translates as "in the manner of a grotto." The reference is to the chambers of ancient Roman buildings uncovered by archeological digs. They often contained murals of a fanciful nature, where combined human and animal forms were portrayed. The element of fantasy was very strong in these pictures, and distortion and exaggeration were the norm.

Ultimately, the word was applied to anything bizarre or absurd—people, events, landscapes, statues, etc. For a while, the British slang term grotty—a derivative of grotesque—referred to something unpleasant or miserable.

The word grotto was a descendent of the Greek verb *kruptein*, to conceal. Thus, crypt, cryptic, encryption, and Kryptonite are kissing cousins.

Q.   Why do they use the word *hound* to describe someone who collects rocks—a rockhound?

A.   The word hound comes from an old Teutonic word meaning a dog. The *Oxford English Dictionary* suggests that ultimately it may come from a verb meaning to seize, thus making the noun mean "the creature that seizes."

As time went on, different strains were promoted to hunt specific animals. Thus, we have the buckhound, deerhound, foxhound, and staghound. The bloodhound doesn't just track blood, of course; scent hound might be more accurate.

ANSWER 30   (B) OVERT

Overt means open and obvious.

Furtive, surreptitious, and clandestine mean secret or stealthy.

As applied to humans, *hound* signifies someone enthusiastic about a pursuit, usually an avid amateur or hobbyist. It is an analogy based on the eagerness and relentless pursuit exhibited by all those working dogs.

You learn what the enthusiast's interest is by focusing on the first element in the word, the one that precedes *-hound*. Common compounds are rock hound, news hound, food hound, and publicity hound. In 1926, *American Speech Magazine* applied the term "comma hound" to composition teachers. And all of my readers are word hounds.

Q. The *National Review* referred to a "fawning *Chicago Tribune* profile of the Obama/Reverend Wright relationship." Why fawning?

A. The verb to fawn probably comes from an obsolete 13th century word meaning to rejoice. The word was applied to the behavior of dogs when they greet their master. There is usually frantic cavorting, whining, and vigorous wags of the tail.

Later, it was applied to humans, but by then it had taken on a pejorative cast. The implication was that the fawning person was servile, abject, cringing, desperate for favor.

Q. I came across a strange word when I was reading *Oliver Twist* for a book report: "The object of this new liking was not among his myrmidons."

A. Great word. Currently, it means a faithful follower, a henchman. The word comes to us through the *Iliad* [2, 684]. The Myrmidons were fierce, war-loving inhabitants of the Isle of Aegina, and Achilles was their leader in the Iliad's time frame.

At one point in their early history, goes the story, the entire population of the island was destroyed by a plague. King Aecus, king of Aegia and son of Zeus, prayed to his father for help. During his prayers, his eyes lit on a nearby ant hill, and he fervently prayed for citizens as numerous as the long line of ants. Zeus transformed those ants into humans, and the island was repopulated. Not by coincidence, the word for ants was *myrmekes*. An expert in ant behavior is known as a myrmecologist.

By Shakespeare's time, the word meant *a member of a bodyguard or retinue; a faithful follower; one of a group or team of*

153

attendants, servants, or assistants. By mid-17th century, it had taken on a negative cast: *a member of a gang or army adhering to a particular leader; a hired ruffian or mercenary.* By the 1800s, myrmidon referred to *an opportunistic or sycophantic supporter; a hanger-on.*

Q.   I'm a big fan of Patrick O'Brian. He sometimes uses a term that I was not familiar with: slab-sided. What can you tell me about that adjective?

A.   Though there isn't unanimity about where the word came from, we all know that a slab is a flat, thick, and broad piece of material, like the slabs of marble used on the face of a public monument. There is agreement that slab-sided involves having long, flat sides, and when applied colloquially to a person, it means that he or she is tall, slim, and lanky.

But the description isn't confined to humans. It also applies to a wide range of objects: sailing ships, guns, chickens, dogs, fish, horses, cars, flat irons, and so on. O'Brian, of course, was referring to ships.

Here's a nonfiction use of the term: "The descendants of the Cape Ann Dory are still raced as the Town Class. Due to their 'V'-shaped hulls, dories have a tendency to heel sharply at first, especially those which were more slab-sided than rounded."

A review of O'Brian's *The Ionian Mission* says this: "After they have reported in and taken their station Stephen Maturin goes into Barcelona with the Dryad, a slab-sided sloop captained by William Babbington, Jack Aubrey's former midshipman."

Q.   I have another eggcorn for you. I heard someone say, "I can't quite phantom what his motives are."

A.   Good catch. That should be fathom, of course. Fathom is a word that served a useful purpose at one time. It started out in Old English as

---

QUICK QUIZ 31

Which one does not belong in this list?

(A) resolute   (B) decrepit   (C) debilitated   (D) fragile

a word to describe a person standing with two arms outstretched. The Dutch formalized it as a measurement of six feet, roughly the distance from fingertips to fingertips when your arms are stretched as wide as they can reach. (Ask any fisherman.)

For centuries, the fathom was the unit of measurement used by sailing ships to take soundings—in other words, to determine the depth of the water under the vessel to prevent grounding. Shakespeare used the word in that maritime sense in *The Tempest*: "Full fadom fiue thy Father lies." [I. ii. 396] The spelling varied through the years, ranging from faethom to vadome to fadome to fawdome and so on.

The idea of measuring the depth of the water was later extended to intellectually delving into, seeing through, and thoroughly understanding someone or something. Fannie Burney used the word in this sense in her *Diary*: "His character I am at this moment unable to fathom." It also showed up in Charlotte Bronte's *Villette*: "I saw something in that lad's eye I never quite fathomed."

It's still a useful verb, even showing up in sporting news headlines: "Dolphins' playoff drought hard to fathom: Dolphins face 5th year in a row with no postseason." [*South Florida Sun-Sentinel*]

Q. How about the use of the phrase "at all". Where did that come from? Here's an example: "Does anyone listen to your show at all?"

A. The *Oxford English Dictionary* tells us that it means in every way, in any way, altogether. Miles Coverdale used it in his 1535 translation of the Bible. "Sayenge: peace, peace, when there is no peace at all." [Jeremiah vi. 14]

It also worked its way into the 1611 Authorized Version of the Bible: "If thy father at all misse me." [1 Samuel xx. 6]

Q. Why do they call it cappuccino?

A. Cappuccino is espresso coffee mixed or topped with steamed milk or cream. In Italy, it is considered a breakfast drink.

It takes its name from the color of a friar's habit, specifically, a Capuchin friar. The cappuccio was the hood attached to the garment. In English, it is spelled capuche.

The patron of the order was St. Francis of Assisi, though the Capuchins weren't established until the 16th century Their habit, floor

155

length and chestnut in color, reflects the fact that St. Francis ordered his monks to wear undyed wool.

Before the variant that designates a type of coffee drink, it was used for the name of a monkey indigenous to Central and South America. The Capuchin monkey has a hoodlike tuft of hair on its head, so a reference to the cappuccio was entirely natural.

Q.   Hunters speak of their quarry. How does that connect to mining operations in a quarry?

A.   Quarry is an interesting word with many meanings. Originally, it referred to scraps given as a reward to successful hunting hounds or to a trained hawk. Eventually, the meaning turned to the victim of the bird of prey or to the animal pursued by a hunter. The base for this word was the Latin *corium*, skin. This word was also applied to a heap of deer piled together at the end of a hunt—the equivalent of our modern buck pole— and to a pile of human bodies. The verb form could refer to training a hawk or hound or to the actions required to track down the prey.

Another word with the same spelling owes its origin to the Latin *quadrare*, to square. It was applied to the open pit from which stones and other building materials were extracted. Obsolete meanings of this word included the hard granular part of a pear, a square-headed arrow, a pane of glass, and a square candle. In all cases, the "fourness" of the original Latin can be discerned. The verb form involves the actions needed to extract building materials

Q.   My mother used to say, "I searched from stem to gudgeon." I never did find out what a gudgeon is. Can you help?

A.   My first reaction was that it sounds like a variation on the far more common "stem to stern," and that turns out to be correct. Before that show was over, listener Charles from Atwood, MI, volunteered that

---

ANSWER 31   (A) RESOLUTE

Resolute means strong and determined.

Decrepit, debilitated, and fragile mean weak.

you might have misheard the word escutcheon as a child, accidentally turning it into gudgeon

An escutcheon was the shield-shaped surface on which a coat of arms was painted. In nautical terms, it was the plate bearing the vessel's name, and it was placed, almost universally, at the back end of the ship—an early version of a license plate. This is confirmed by *Smyth's Sailor's Word Book*, 1867, which placed the escutcheon smack dab in the middle of the ship's stern

But the word gudgeon actually exists; it is not just a corruption of escutcheon. The *Oxford English Dictionary* has this: "Nautical: A metal socket in which the pintle of a rudder turns." That sent me scrambling to find pintle, which the OED defines as, "A pin forming part of the hinge of a rudder, usually fixed on the rudder and fitting into a ring on the sternpost."

The stem, of course, was the curved upright timber at the bow of a vessel, so whether you use stem to stern, stem to gudgeon, or stem to escutcheon, the meaning is from front to back.

Q. Where did sunbeam come from?

A. Sunbeam is a warm, comfort-filled word, but quirky nonetheless. It is, of course, a ray of sunshine, so the sun- segment makes perfect sense, but what about a beam? I associate that with the huge piece of timber used in construction to hold up the roof.

As it turns out, so did the scholar who invented the word. We're talking about Alfred the Great, famous for building up the storehouse of Old English literature by translating books from Latin.

While he was translating Bede's *Historia ecclesiastica gentis Anglorum* (*Ecclesiastical History of the English People*), he kept bumping up against the image *columna lucis*, rendered as "column of light" in modern English. Old English did not contain the word column, so Alfred reached for the nearest reality in his day: bêam, a tree or building post.

So a sunbeam was a sun post was a columna lucis.

Q. My English teacher says that we shouldn't use blatant and flagrant interchangeably. What do you think?

A.   Are you trying to get me in trouble? Blatant and flagrant are often treated as synonyms, something that throws language purists into conniption fits. "Conspicuously reprehensible" sums up the shared meaning.

The American Heritage Dictionary prefers blatant if you are referring to the shameless in-your-face nature of the act, and flagrant if you are emphasizing the serious moral failure at the heart of the act.

Blatant is a word that was either invented or adapted by Edmund Spenser in his *Fairie Queene*. There's a remote chance that it was related to the word bleating, and it may owe its existence to the Latin *blatire*, to babble. Today, it is a word that depends upon sight, but originally, it related to the auditory sense. In fact, for a couple of centuries, its sole meaning was noisy or clamorous.

Flagrant owes its existence to the Latin *flagrare*, to burn. Glowing, fiery, and hot were the original meanings, but by the 18th century, it had taken on the sense of notorious or scandalous.

If you are prone to outbursts of censoriousness, there are other fine words at your disposal: atrocious, audacious, brazen, disgraceful, flagitious, glaring, gross, heinous, monstrous, nefarious, outrageous, rank, scandalous, and shocking. I can feel the temperature rising.

Q.   It seems to be politically incorrect to use the word these days, but where did the word lunatic come from?

A.   While lunatic is used to designate a crazy or very foolish person, these days we use a much softened sense of this word. "He's a lunatic" can be said with fondness and admiration; think Bill Murray.

A few centuries back, lunatic and insane were a technical pair. Insanity was a permanent condition, chronic in nature. Lunacy was intermittent; there were periods of lucidity.

But what triggered the bouts of lunacy? The ancient Romans thought they knew: it was the phases of the moon. A waxing moon brought lucidity; a full moon brought out the wolf man in us.

And the Latin word for moon? It was *luna*, of course.

QUICK QUIZ 32

Which one does not belong in this list?

(A) intractable   (B) compliant   (C) recalcitrant   (D) refractory

Q.   What can you tell me about the word knapsack?

A.   This word figures prominently in the song *Happy Wanderer*, a German import sung by generations of American Scouts.

> "I love to go a-wanderin
> Along the mountain track.
> And as I go, I love to sing,
> My knapsack on my back."

The –sack half of the word is obvious. Americans tend to use the word backpack, but it's the same convenient carrier.

The history of the knack- portion is a bit less obvious, but according to the *Oxford English Dictionary*, it seems to come from German and/or Dutch words meaning to eat or to bite. Those words, in turn, came from an earlier word meaning to crack something or to chip a stone. The implication, therefore, is that it's the kind of eating where you bite off small pieces of something, rather than sitting down to a sumptuous dinner.

So the knapsack was a snack sack—food on the run.

Q.   One of my favorite TV programs is *Jeopardy* (I'm sure you watch it, too), but I was wondering why it has such an extreme name. Jeopardy is a life-and-death sort of situation.

A.   True enough, today jeopardy is a relentlessly one-sided word. It screams danger and peril, the possibility of losing life, property, reputation, freedom, or anything else that we prize.

But when the word started, it was less one-sided; it was more balanced and equitable. In Old French, it was *geu parti*, and it meant a divided game, divided in the sense of a 50/50 chance for either side to win.

It involved a game that depended upon strategy, such as chess, a game that could go either way. The *geu* segment derived from the Latin *jocus*, a jest or a joke. No one's life was in danger.

By the 14th century, jeopardy had picked up the univocal sense of risk and danger, a radical departure from its original meaning.

Q.   I play the saxophone myself, but I just found out today in band practice that fulcrum is a term used in drumming. I always thought it was from physics.

A.   I didn't know that. I dabbled in guitar as a teenager, but I became unstrung.

A fulcrum is defined as the point or support on which a lever pivots. I, too, always associated it with classical physics, probably because of Archimedes' famous boast: "Give me a place to stand and with a lever I will move the whole world." That place to stand would have been his fulcrum.

However, according to the origin of the word, Archimedes could have saved his energy and stayed in bed. The Latin verb *fulcire* meant to support or prop up, which fits in nicely with the fulcrum/lever image.

But when the noun fulcrum developed from that verb, it had a quite specific meaning. It meant a bed or couch post or foot. There were usually four of them, and their function was to raise the bed or couch from the drafty floor. It's a great example of how words may change their meanings over the centuries.

Q.   Foolhardy strikes me as another one of those words that is self-contradictory. Hardy means strong and secure, but that gets cancelled out by fool.

A.   Hardy also means rash and presumptuous, and that's why it was paired with fool in this word [1225].

A fool is a simpleton, someone who acts in a stupid manner, a person deficient in intelligence or judgment. The explosive -f- at the start of the word helps to make it sound like a contemptuous insult.

It started out as the Latin word *follis*, a bellows. Bellows are used to increase the heat of a fire by force-feeding it oxygen. In a portable bellows, two projections are grasped, one in each hand, and with a pumping motion, air enters one end of the bellows, is compressed in a

> ### Answer 32   (B) compliant
>
> Compliant means agreeable, disposed to cooperate.
>
> Intractable, recalcitrant, and refractory mean stubborn and uncooperative.

(usually) leather bag, and is expelled forcefully through a nozzle. To a blacksmith, it is an essential tool.

In the Late Latin era, the word was extended to mean a windbag or an airhead — therefore, a fool. As William Caxton put it in 1481, "There ben more fooles than wysemen."

Q. I can't believe the range of meanings that the word delirious has. At one end of the spectrum, it means mentally disordered, incoherent, not making sense. At the other end, it means wildly happy.

A. Focus on that "wildly"; it's a hyperbolic step away from "out of your mind." Curiously, the word comes to us from the field of agriculture—literally. In Latin, a *lira* was the ridge between two furrows. A furrow is the narrow trench made in the earth with a plow, especially for the reception of seed. Setting plants in parallel lines is an efficient way to maximize available space.

To go *de lira* (away from the direction of the furrow) was to begin plowing in a crooked line, to deviate from the straight path.

So the word denoting a confused mental state started out as the act of a careless or inattentive farmer

Q. I've been reading *Tom Sawyer* with my children, and we've come across a word that has us stymied: maow. Was that a slang term in Mark Twain's day?

A. Actually, it's a case of imitative spelling. Let's take a fast look at the word in context:

The night promised to be a fair one; so Tom went home with the understanding that if a considerable degree of darkness came on, Huck was to come and "maow," whereupon he would slip out and try the keys. [Ch. XXVIII]

'All you got to do is to trot up Hooper Street a block and maow — and if I'm asleep, you throw some gravel at the window and that'll fetch me." [Ch. XXVIII]

"Well, if I don't want you in the daytime, I'll let you sleep. I won't come bothering around. Any time you see something's up, in the night, just skip right around and maow." [Ch. XXVIII]

Tom's excitement enabled him to keep awake until a pretty late hour, and he had good hopes of hearing Huck's "maow," and of having his treasure to astonish Becky and the picnickers with, next day; but he was disappointed. No signal came that night. [Ch. XXIX]

So "maow" is a vocal signal worked out by the boys. It's an imitation of the sound that a cat would make, the kind of sound that wouldn't alarm a casual listener or betray the boys' presence. In our day, we're more likely to spell it meow

Q. "I can't determine if "molly cat" refers to a promiscuous cat or to a promiscuous woman. Any ideas?"

A. The words moll or molly derive from the name Mary. In Britain, if the original name contained an "r", it was common for the nickname to contain an "l". Prince Harold became Prince Hal; Sarah became Sally.

Consider an early 20th century use: gun moll. The second word designated a disreputable woman. In fact, going back to 1604, it was a synonym for a prostitute. A moll house was a house of prostitution.

Similarly, by analogy to the freewheeling feline, cat is a slang word for a prostitute. Clients in a cat house are catting around.

So using the information above, you'll be able to observe the term molly cat in context to see if it refers to a promiscuous cat or to a loose-living woman who is catting around.

Q. Increasingly, I have been seeing the spelling *grievious* instead of *grievous*. Is it changing?

A. The word has two syllables, grievous; the *–i-* simply doesn't belong. This falls Into the category known as an eggcorn, a term invented by Mark Lieberman in September 2003 on his *Language Log*.

It referred to a regional dialect that rendered *acorn* as *eggcorn*. The result is a mistake that gets enshrined as correct and even acquires defenders. You'll see *centrifical force* instead of *centrifugal*, came through with *flying collars* instead of *colors*, *give reign* to emotions instead of *give rein*, *tow* the line instead of *toe* the line, *nerve-wrecking* instead of *nerve-wracking*, a *bowl* in a china shop, *gingervitis*, and my favorite, she drank herself into *Bolivia*.

Q. When Obama gave that speech about his white grandmother making racist remarks, Republican critics were quick to say that he had thrown his grandmother under the bus. What's the origin of the phrase?

A. "To throw someone under the bus" (or "under the wheels") means to reject or betray someone, to treat someone as a scapegoat, or to put someone out of favor or at a disadvantage.

The first citation that I have found was attributed to David Remnick of the *Washington Post* (Sept. 7, 1984): *Pensive,With Orange Hair Cyndi Lauper & Her Tunes on Tour*: "In the rock 'n' roll business, you are either on the bus or under it. Playing "Feelings" with Eddie and the Condos in a buffet bar in Butte is under the bus. Peter Frampton is under the bus. God willing, so are the Bee Gees."

Q. I've been wondering about the horse in horseradish. The only thing that makes sense to me is that in German it is Meersrettich (sea radish). Meer is phonetically identical to "mare" or a female horse, so I think that horseradish was based on a misconception; people thought *horse* instead of *sea*.

A. From what I've read, this won't hold water. The Meer in the German version actually meant *more* or *greater*, relating to its size or to its strong aroma. This is reflected in the French word for radish, *raifort*, which seems to have come from the Latin *radis fort*, strong radish. One of the early uses in English (1597, Gerarde's *Herbal II*) also reflects this: "Horse Radish bringeth foorth great leaues."

Q. Where does hoity-toity come from?

A. It's easier to say what it means. Currently, it means pompous or full of pretentious airs. Earlier (17th c.), it meant frivolous, riotous, and flighty. It was applied to someone who played the fool.

The *Oxford English Dictionary* points to a connection with *hoyden*, a rude, ill-bred, and noisy girl. In turn, that is connected with the dialectical *hoit*, riotous and noisy mirth.

At one point, it was also spelled highty-tighty, with a reference to someone being high and mighty. Dickens (*Martin Chuzzlewit*) and Thackery (*Vanity Fair*) both used that spelling, as well as the other. In both cases, reduplication is at work.

Snopes.com dismisses the rumor that it comes from the French *haut toit*, high roof, because the supercilious look down on others.

Q.   Where did "to rob Peter to pay Paul" come from?

A.   A popular explanation found on the internet is that it arose during the reign of Edward VI, when, in 1540, the lands of St. Peter at Westminster were appropriated to raise money for the repair of St. Paul's in London.

The problem is the timeline. The phrase was already in existence 200 years earlier and was used by Wycliffe. Christine Ammer thinks that it may be a transmutation of a 12th century expression: *"Tanquam si quis Crucifigeret Paulum ut redimeret Petrum"* (as it were that one would crucify Paul in order to redeem Peter). Oddly enough, the cadence and the basic idea show up in a number of languages:

- French: to strip Peter to clothe Paul.
- Spanish: to undress one saint to dress another.
- German: to take from Peter and give to Paul.
- Italian: to strip the altar cloths from one altar to cover another.
- Chinese: to tear something apart and use the pieces to fix something else.

Q.   My grandmother used to say that I was "out of sorts" when I was being bratty or peevish. Where did that come from?

A.   Traditionally, it meant not being in your usual good health or spirits, usually accompanied by physical discomfort. One of the many meanings of *sort* was character, disposition, or rank. So when you are out of sorts, you have slipped from your usual disposition or character.

A parallel phrase that developed was "out of humor." In ancient medicine, the four humors were essential bodily fluids. When they were in balance, everything was healthy. When they became unbalanced—out

---

QUICK QUIZ 33

Which one does not belong in this list?

(A) ephemeral   (B) evanescent   (C) transitory   (D) immutable

of humor—physical or mental health was jeopardized, and you didn't seem to be the same person.

"Out of sorts" seems always to involve a loss, not a gain. In other words, if you are negative and pessimistic by nature, being out of sorts will not make you positive and optimistic. It's not used in that direction.

I should mention that there is some disagreement connected with the origin of *out of sorts*. Brewer's *Dictionary of Phrase and Fable* mentions three competing theories:

- Sorts was a name for any particular letter used by typographers. So if a printer was "out of sorts," he couldn't finish his printing job unless he substituted another letter.
- "The French *être dérangé* explains the metaphor. If cards are out of sorts they are deranged, and if a person is out of sorts, the health or spirits are out of order."
- "The French *ne pas être dans son assiette* explains the metaphor." (He's not on his plate.) *Assiette*, aside from meaning sorts, was a plate. Picture a plate of vegetables or hors d'ouevres at a party. If a piece of carrot falls to the floor, it is out of its proper place; it is out of sorts.

These don't strike me as definitive, but I'm open to documentation.

Q. Where did we get, "what's all this kamalya about?" It was used frequently in my family many years ago.

A. I don't have a definitive answer for this one. However, I found something that strikes me as more than mere coincidence. There was an influential American composer, musical theorist, and publisher named Henry Cowell [1897–1965]. Critic Virgil Thompson wrote this in the early 1950s:

"Henry Cowell's music covers a wider range in both expression and technique than that of any other living composer. His experiments begun three decades ago in rhythm, in harmony, and in instrumental sonorities were considered then by many to be wild.... No other composer of our time has produced a body of works so radical and so normal, so penetrating and so comprehensive."

Notice that his works were characterized as wild and radical. In 1939, his piece named Comallya was released. I haven't heard it performed, but if it was wild and radical, that might explain, "What's all this comallya about?"

Q.   I notice that the term oxbow is used frequently on maps, as in Oxbow Lake. Why?

A.   Variant forms of ox, the word referring to the large ruminant animal, are found early on in Old Frisian, Old Dutch, Old Saxon, Old Icelandic, Old Swedish, Danish, Gothic, and so on. It's a testimony to the importance of the animal in agricultural use in northern climes.

A bow is something bent or fashioned so as to form part of the circumference of a circle or other curve; it's a bend, or a bent line.

An oxbow was a bow-shaped piece of wood forming a collar for a yoked ox, with the upper ends fastened to the yoke. In 18th century America, it was used to designate a pronounced meander or horseshoe-shaped loop in a river. It was also applied to a lake formed from an oxbow in a river when it silted up and became an enclosed body of water — a lake.

Q.   On the stock market, why are the animal metaphors of bear and bull used?

A.   Jason Zweig of *Money Magazine* says that the origins of these terms are not clear. But there are some possibilities.

In the 18th century, bearskin traders often sold the skins before even catching the bears. It was an aggressive approach, but the quantity and quality of any skins that might be found was dubious; it could lead to a weak trading environment and a poorly performing market beset by uncertainty. Zweig cites an admonitory proverb of the times: "Don't sell the bearskin before you've killed the bear."

The style of a bull was to charge forward with force, as does a favorable market when prices escalate. Frederick Jackson wrote this in

> ## Answer 33   (D) immutable
>
> Immutable means unchangeable.
>
> Ephemeral, evanescent, and transitory mean temporary.

1841 in his *A Week in Wall Street by One Who Knows*: "A bull is a man who has more shares than he can keep and has gored his neighbor to procure them."

Q.   I need to know whether these four sentences should end with a period or a question mark.

A.   Here are the four sentences and my advice.

1) *I might conclude, when has it not been so?*
        The last part of the sentence is a direct question. The opening statement acts merely as its introduction.
2) *It seems we spent an awful lot of time dancing, doesn't it?*
        Same reason: the last part of the sentence is a direct question.
3) *It's funny, isn't it, that although we've grown up together, we have nothing in common.*
        Ends with a period. The embedded question (*isn't it*) is parenthetical. If you were to leave it out, the sentence would still make sense.
4) *We hopped on board the bus, and, wouldn't you know it, ended up going in the wrong direction.*
        Ends with a period for the same reason: the embedded question (*wouldn't you know it*) is parenthetical. If you were to leave it out, the sentence would still make sense.

Q.   Why do we refer to some people or institutions as fly-by-night?

A.   Today, it means any kind of disreputable or illegal activity, especially if the perpetrator begins making excuses or takes off as soon as the foul deed is done.
        Before that, it was used when a tenant would vacate his lodgings in the middle of the night to avoid paying his landlord or other creditors.
        And originally, in the late 18th century, it was a term of reproach to a woman signifying that she was a witch who took off on nightly rides on her broom.

Q.   What is the origin of the word fascist?

A. It turns out to be only a little bit better than a stick in the eye. Fascist comes from the Latin word fasces, a bundle of sticks. It was a symbol of the power of Roman magistrates, whose duty was to preserve and dispense justice.

A bundle of rods was tied tightly around an axe and carried before the magistrate by his Lictors. They acted as his bodyguards and as instruments of justice: they could beat an offender with rods if the magistrate so ordered, or they could behead the most serious perpetrators.

There was also a symbolic value to the fasces. They stood for strength through unity. You could easily snap a single rod, but a bound bundle was impervious. So, too, the Roman Republic — a tightly-bound alliance of citizens and allies — could face its enemies with confidence and power.

In time, the concept degenerated into the dark side of power: oppression, use of sheer force to impose will, and a system that crushed state-defined decadent individuals and organizations in order to promote a new national purity.

In our day, it has often been watered down to become a synonym for a bully.

Q. What is the opposite of an epiphany?

A. An interesting question. First, let's deal with epiphany. In the ancient world, according to myths, epics, and religious works, an epiphany occurred when a god or goddess chose to reveal itself to a mere mortal. Above all, in the ancient world, it was meant to be evidence that the human hero or leader was worthy of knowledge, power, or credibility. It was a compelling endorsement of his or her mission, message, or destiny. Epihany came from two Greek terms: *epi-*, to, and *phanein*, to show. Thus, it was a manifestation, a deliberate and directed revelation, and an inspiring or instigative appearance.

In the Christian religion, The Epiphany is a specific festival: the manifestation of Christ to the Gentiles in the person of the Magi. In

---

Quick Quiz 34

Which one does not belong in this list?

(A) caustic   (B) mordant   (C) complimentary   (D) sardonic the Western Church, the feast is celebrated on January 6. The account may be found in Matthew 2: 1 - 12. Another important New Testament epiphany occurs in the account of Jesus' baptism.

In time, epiphany was secularized and democratized and came to mean any flash of insight, any sudden intuitive realization. It no longer needed a god or goddess; it had moved to the internal forum.

To get back to the original question: what is the opposite of an epiphany? Frankly, I've had difficulty finding a word endorsed by widespread usage. Jung used the term anti-epiphany. I haven't dipped into his works since the 1970s, but at the risk of distortion and simplification, I have a hazy memory that it was a defense mechanism to prevent an overload of information and revelation. Some things it's better not to realize; blocking—at least on a temporary basis—isn't always negative.

So, let me approach the question from an etymological perspective. An epiphany leads a person to a burst of internal light. We need a term to metaphorically express leading a person to a dark cave. Let's save the *epi-*, meaning to, and let's add the combining form -calyptry, from the Greek kalyptra, covered and hidden as by a veil. Thus, we have epicalyptry [ep´-ee-cal-ip´-tree], deliberate concealment from self or resistance to insight. Spread the word, folks. Let's get it into dictionaries.

Q. "The word I'm asking about is 'bogus.' *Merriam-Webster* yields little other than *pertaining to counterfeit money and the apparatus used to print counterfeit money* (1825). I have to think that the origin of this word is based upon an acronym, the last two letters standing for United States. The third letter might well refer to 'government' and perhaps the second is 'of.' Tell me what the 'B' represents or tell me that my logic sucks and indicate where this word really began."

A. Let's see: B.O.G.U.S. = Bull**** of the Government of the United States? That's about as convincing as the Ship High In Transit story to explain manure.

For the most part, acronyms (words formed from first letters of each word and pronounced as a word —NATO) did not exist before 1900, so we can rule that out.

Originally, bogus was the name for a counterfeit coin, but no one is sure why. The first appearance in print, according to *The Random House Historical Dictionary of American Slang*, was 1797 in a book called *Band of Brothers*: "Coney means Counterfeit paper money . . . Bogus means spurious coin."

Another appearance in print is very detailed. We have an account from Eber D. Howe, editor of the *Painsville Telegraph* (Painesville, Ohio) in 1827. A group of counterfeiters was arrested in May of that year as a large crowd watched. When a confiscated machine used to stamp out phony coins was carried out of the building, someone in the crowd shouted, "That's a bogus!"

Eber D Howe speculated that it was a shortened version of tantrabogus, a word he knew from his childhood and which in his father's time back in Vermont meant any ill-looking object. Michael Quinion (*World Wide Words*) suggests that it might be linked to the old Devonshire dialect word tantarabobs, a word for the devil or any misshapen creature, making it a relative of words like bogy and boogie man.

Another theory traces "bogus" to "boko," which means "fake" in the West African Hausa language. Perhaps slaves brought it over, is the suggestion. Word expert Eric Partridge (*A Dictionary of Slang and Unconventional English*) suggests that it might be connected to the 18th c. [1758] callibogus, an inferior beverage composed of cheap rum and spruce beer or other liquor or molasses. It's a tradition in Newfoundland.

Q.   Should the word be spelled chaperon or chaperone?

A.   Both are found in dictionaries, but some commentators point out that the chaperone spelling is an incorrect Anglicization of a French word. Someone mistakenly thought that an -e- was needed at the end of the word to make it feminine. So it's probably better to give preference to chaperon.

More interesting is its origin. It comes from an Old French word that meant a hood used to cover a person's head protectively. *The American Heritage Dictionary* also points out that it was applied to the hood placed on a hawk's head to keep it calm.

ANSWER 34   (D) IMMUTABLE

Complimentary means flattering.

Caustic, mordent, and sardonic mean biting or critical.

In a strange turn of events, it also meant a small escutcheon placed on the forehead of a horse pulling a hearse during a funeral procession. [1680]

By 1720, the transfer from a protective head covering to a protective person was complete. By then, it meant "a married or elderly woman, who, for the sake of propriety, accompanies a young unmarried lady in public as guide and protector." [*OED*]

Q. Words like schizophrenic, oligophrenic, etc., have the same origin and apparently derive from the Greek "*phren*", meaning mind. However, in medicine, phrenic also refers to the diaphragm (the phrenic nerve, for example, is the nerve controlling the diaphragm).

Is there an ancient connection between the two, that is, between the location of the diaphragm and the mind? I performed a search on the internet and could not find an explanation for this use of the same word for apparently such different concepts.

A. As often happens, extension of meaning accounts for the confusion. The Greek -*phren*- had a range of meanings, at first applying principally to the mind or will. But we must realize that the seat of the mind for some Greek philosophers was not the physical brain, but the heart. Their view of mind and emotion was cardiocentric.

Some ancient Greek theoreticians believed that an inflammation of the diaphragm was responsible for mental disorders, so the meaning encapsulated in -*phren*- was extended to the midriff, diaphragm, or area surrounding the heart. Thus, the seat of all the -*phrenia* or -*phrenic* words was the diaphragm, where, as you point out, the phrenic nerve is to be found.

Let's look at some of the interesting -*phrenic* words.
- electrophrenic: involving or designating electrical stimulation of the phrenic nerves.
- gastrophrenic: pertaining to the stomach and to the diaphragm
- hebephrenic: relating to a form of insanity incident to the age of puberty
- idiophrenic: relating to a form of insanity which is caused by disease of the brain itself (1886)
- oligophrenic: of, relating to, or exhibiting mental retardation

- paraphrenia: relating to mental illness with prominent paranoid or other delusional symptoms; paranoid schizophrenia
- phrenic: supplying the diaphragm; of, relating to, or affecting the diaphragm; diaphragmatic
- quantophrenic: relating to undue reliance on or use of facts that can be quantified or analysed using mathematical or statistical methods; inappropriate application of such methods, esp. in the fields of sociology and anthropology (1956)
- schizophrenic: relating to a mental disorder occurring in various forms, all characterized by a breakdown in the relation between thoughts, feelings, and actions, usually with a withdrawal from social activity and the occurrence of delusions and hallucinations

[Source: *Oxford English Dictionary*]

Q.   I'm wondering about the history of the word bribe.

A.   Start by thinking of bread. Today, a bribe is money or a favor given to a person of some authority in order to influence his or her decision. The word started out in Old French as a piece of bread, particularly one given to a beggar. As time went on, it began to refer to a professional beggar, often unsavory, who lived on alms. From there, it became plunder or spoils, and it was applied to the person who received them. Somewhere in the 16th century, direction shifted, and it became an act of the giver.

There are a couple of other common words based on bread. A companion is a buddy, an associate, a comrade. Literally, a companion is someone with whom you share bread (L. *com*, together, and *panis*, bread). Comrade, by the way, means a chamber-mate, someone who shares a tent with you. We can see the early military contexts involved in companion and comrade.

Then there's canister, a small metal container used to hold tea, coffee, and other food items, but it started out in Latin (*canistrum*) with a very specific meaning: a bread basket. You might keep your canisters in a pantry, a closet or small room in the kitchen used to store food items, utensils, and other cooking and eating aids. Originally, it was a storeroom for bread (*panis*).

Q. Did you know that the sporting term upset—an unexpected defeat by an underdog—goes back to horse racing? The famous Man o' War was beaten by a horse named Upset!

A. Hold your horses; I wouldn't bet on that one. True, the defeat is a matter of racing history. At the Sanford Memorial Stakes, held on August 13, 1919, Upset won by half a length after Man o' War got boxed in by other horses.

The issue is, is that where we got the word upset referring to unexpected results in a sporting event, an election, or any other type of contest? This provides us with an opportunity to review a basic principle of etymology: precedence does matter. In other words, if someone claims that a term originated in 1919, but evidence shows that it existed earlier, the claim cannot stand.

A classic example is the belief that the word hooker, referring to a prostitute, originated with Civil War General Joseph Hooker and his lusty regiment. If true, that would put the origin somewhere between 1861 - 1865. But it shows up as early as September 1835 in *The New York Transcript*, and in 1845 in N.E. Eliason's *Tarheel Talk*. The good General and his antics may have reinforced the use of the word, but it wasn't named after him as legend would have it.

But I digress; back to upset. Meaning an overturning or overthrow, it dates back to 1822. That's exactly what happens in an unexpected victory: the favorite is overturned, overthrown, defeated. The horse was named for this idea, not the other way around. Perhaps Upset, the horse, deepened the use of the word, but he didn't invent it.

By the way, the same is true for Man o' War. In 1449, it meant a soldier. By 1484, it was a commissioned naval warship. The name Man o' War was chosen by its owner's wife (Mrs. Eleanor Robson Belmont) to honor her husband's service in World War I. It was meant to provoke the idea of a formidable opponent.

Q. Winter will soon be here in the Great North, so I was wondering about the word blizzard.

A. The Weather Channel website tells us that the following requirements are necessary to speak of a blizzard:
- temperatures below 20 degrees Fahrenheit
- winds of 35 miles per hour or greater

- falling or blowing snow in the air that reduces visibility to ¼ mile or less
- a duration of at least 3 hours

Originally, blizzard meant a violent blow; then it came to mean an overwhelming argument. The first print instance cited by the *Oxford English Dictionary* appeared in 1829: "Blizzard: a violent blow." [*Virginia Lit. Museum*, Dec. 16, 1829, p. 418]

By 1859, the transfer from a punch to a snow squall had been completed: "A blizzard had come upon us about midnight... Shot 7 horses that were so chilled could not get up." [L. B. Wolf, *Diary*, Dec. 1, 1859, in *Kansas Historical Quarterly* (1932), I. 205]

Metaphorically, it has come to mean a flurry of activity or a superabundance: a blizzard of phone calls, a blizzard of spam.

Q. Where do we get the expression *dire straights*?

A. It's a frequent misconception that the second word is spelled *straight*. I've also seen this in the phrase *a straight jacket*. There's nothing straight about it in these cases. It should be spelled strait.

Strait came from *estreit*, an Old French word that meant tight, close, or narrow. In turn, that evolved from the Latin word *strictus*, which meant drawn together, close-knit, tight, or narrow.

In 1387, strait was used to describe a tight-fitting garment. By 1561, it referred to a constraining knot. As time went on, limited or constricted was the predominant meaning, leading to the idea of difficult. We find it in Matthew 7:14: "Because strait is the gate, and narrow is the way, which leadeth unto life, and few there be that find it." [*KJV*] It became applied to a narrow waterway, often with a plural spelling treated as a singular: the Straits of Hormuz.

Dire came from the Latin *dirus* — fearful, awful, portentous, or ill-boding. In time, it took on shades of unpleasant or frightful. By now, dire straits is considered a cliché.

Q. TV commentators discussing Hurricane Ike kept using the word landfall. I'm familiar with snowfall and rainfall, where the elements literally fall from the sky, but doesn't a hurricane approach horizontally?"

A.   If you ever have a chance to look up the word **fall** in an unabridged dictionary, be prepared to spend some time wading through details. The idea of gravity at work is primary, of course, but one of the subsequent meanings is, "to come upon or arrive."

The original use of landfall referred to a ship arriving at a plotted course. We find this in 1627 in Captain Smith's *Seaman's Grammar*, ix. 43: "A good Land fall is when we fall iust with our reckoning, if otherwise a bad Land fall."

When the Aviation Age arrived, the word was also applied to a plane arriving at land after a flight over the sea. (1908, H. G. Wells, *War in Air* vi. 194: "New York had risen out of the blue indistinctness of the landfall.") By 1974, landfall was also being applied to the place where an undersea pipeline reaches land.

Q.   Do you have information on *feeding frenzy*? I am seeing it a lot in newspapers recently.

A.   That's probably because of the naming of Sarah Palin as the Republic Vice-Presidential candidate.

The original feeding frenzy was the frantic and aggressive attack on prey by groups of sharks, leading to thrashing and writhing bodies in bloody waters. It was a group smorgasbord. The first instance given by the *Oxford English Dictionary* is, "When sharks are in a feeding frenzy, the man who hangs too close to the surface to grimace, may lose his head — face, grimace and all." [T. Lineweaver in *Sports Illustrated*, 22 Feb. 61/2]

Sharks gather when they smell the blood or the stress hormones of potential prey. Research shows that sharks are able to respond to one part blood for every one million parts of water; this is like being able to smell one teaspoon of cherry syrup in a swimming pool.

Eventually, it became a figure of speech for aggressive competition or rivalry, or for exploitation by journalists when they sense a story about to emerge—they smell blood in the water. The first instance of this figurative use found in the *Oxford English Dictionary* is from 1972 [*Science* 7 Apr. 33/3] : "It would be rash to take them [*sc.* proposed alterations to pollution legislation] as evidence of a coherent movement to cripple the law. But what worries environmentalists . . . is that a feeding frenzy may develop among federal agencies once a few loopholes have been opened in the law."

Q. In the financial section of yesterday's newspaper, an economics professor wrote that people lack **numeracy**. From the context, I gather that it means they stink at math, but when did it become a word?

A. The first instance that I can find is from 1959. It was used in a report by an Advisory Council for Education commissioned by the British Ministry of Education: "When we say that a historian or a linguist is 'innumerate' we mean that he cannot even begin to understand what scientists and mathematicians are talking about... It is perhaps possible to distinguish two different aspects of numeracy that should concern the Sixth Former." (In America, that would be the equivalent of the junior and senior years in high school.)

It was built on the model of *literacy*, which evolved from *literate*. Numeracy evolved from *numerate*, an adjective meaning skilled at math. That, in turn, came from *number* with the *-ate* suffix thrown in. Rather than focusing on esoteric math, numeracy seems now to be concerned with the math needed in everyday life. Think compound interest or the stock market, for instance. In fact, many commentators are careful to separate the terms numeracy and mathematics.

At the root of *literacy* is a Latin word meaning letter; the Latin root behind *number* means a sum or numeral. In no time at all, we'll be dealing with historacy and chemistracy.

Q. David Denby's review of WALL-E (*The New Yorker*, July 21, 2008) contains this description: ". . . squadrons of square-shouldered helots who try to squash the slightest sign of free will." Let's hear it for sibilance.

A. Helos was a town in Laconia. Some of its inhabitants were bound in a permanent condition of serfdom. They were suspended between outright slavery and free citizenship. They were permanently inferior, and they were called helots.

Plutarch referred to an odd practice. On certain occasions, helots were compelled to get drunk in public. The idea was that this would instill repugnance towards drunkenness in Spartan youths. I don't know about the success of the maneuver. Today, given the *Kollegians on Kegs* videos, I suspect that it might backfire.

In 19th century biology, helotism was "a form of symbiosis in which one organism makes use of another as if it were a slave, by causing it to function to its own advantage; used esp. of the relationship of the fungus and alga in a lichen by those who regard it as neither mutualism nor parasitism." [*Oxford English Dictionary*]

Q.   What can you tell me about *give it a whirl*, which I take it to mean, give it a try?

A.   It's an American colloquialism and dates back to the late 1800s. It means an attempt, especially an initial or tentative attempt. It has cousins in "give it a shot" and "give it the old college try."

The questioner thought that that it might come from dancing, where a whirling motion is often a prominent feature. Think *Dancing with the Stars* or any Strauss waltz. "Give it a whirl" also conjures up images of a whirling dervish.

As it turns out, it probably has a less festive source. It is likely that it refers to a flywheel. A flywheel is a wheel with a heavy rim attached to a rotating shaft. It may have a variety of purposes: to start a piston engine, to minimize wobble in a machine once it has started, or to collect kinetic power from the rotary motion. In early tractors, for instance, you started the engine by giving a good twist to the flywheel.

So *to give something a whirl* originally was to try to start it up. The *OED* tells us that in Australia and New Zealand, the same idea was expressed by "give it a burl" or "give it a birl." The verb **to birl** always included the idea of rotary motion, whether it spoke of a rifle bullet, a grist mill, or a flipped coin.

Q.   I heard a word on cable TV that I can't find in my dictionary. The word was subitize, and it was used in reference to a bird that could count objects.

A.   This one comes from psychology, but it has worked its way into math discussions. A noun version, subitization, has also been formed. It means to correctly perceive the exact number in a small set without actually counting. The Italian word *subito* means "at once," and it is a descendant of the Latin *subitus*, sudden and unexpected.

The *Oxford English Dictionary* tells us precisely where the word came from in a 1949 citation of E. L. KAUFMAN et al. in *American Journal of Psychology*, LXII. 520: "A new term is needed for the discrimination of stimulus-numbers of 6 and below... The term proposed is subitize... We are indebted to Dr. Cornelia C. Coulter, the Department of Classical Languages and Literatures, Mount Holyoke College, for suggesting this term."

Here is the word in context:

"The infantile sense of numbers is restricted to collections of only four or five objects, and the data suggests that infants and adults manipulate such collections using a mental process quite distinct from counting. For small collections, both adults and infants perceive the "numerosity" of the collection directly, somewhat like we perceive shape or color. This direct, intuitive perception of numerosity is called subitization, and it is the first number skill that we develop. When we see three objects, we don't count "one, two, three," instead we are simply aware of the group's "threeness." Most people can subitize up to seven or eight objects, switching to a variety of counting strategies for larger collections." [*Number Blindness: A Hidden Challenge for Mathematics* by Ashish Ranpura]

Q.   I've always associated the word rude with lack of manners, but in a novel I'm reading, it seems to be a synonym for illiterate.

A.   Except for one or two archaic turns, the word rude has remained consistently negative through the centuries. It derives from the Latin *rudis*, which meant unwrought, unpolished, unformed, inexperienced, or untrained.

It has bounced around as uncultured, ignorant, unrefined, uncivil, lacking in refinement, and downright primitive. It shares a root with its polar opposite, erudite— scholarly, well-instructed, intelligent. Erudite is formed from the Latin *e-*, out or away from, and *rudis*, untrained, etc.

Also in the family is the word rudiments, the basic things taught when a subject is first approached. The adjective form is rudimentary, which Sherlock Holmes could have used instead of "Elementary, my dear Watson." [Yes, I know that the line came from a stage or movie version rather than from Conan Doyle himself, but it's germane.]

Over the centuries, we have lost rudeful (full of rudeness), rudery (act of rudeness), rudesby (a rude fellow), rudeship (roughness), rudish (somewhat rude), and rudesse and rudity (rudeness).

Q.   What's the connection between the color jet black and an aircraft?

A.   Jet black does not refer to dark clouds of smoke billowing from airplane engines. As it turns out, jet has a rich variety of meanings.

The jet in *jet black* refers to a hard compact black form of coal capable of receiving a brilliant polish. In the Middle Ages, it was considered a cure for fevers and for other illnesses. You had to burn it to make it work. It is now used to make toys, buttons, and personal ornaments, and it has the property of attracting light bodies when electrified by rubbing. As a color word, it also applies to marble.

As 18th century slang, jet designated either a lawyer or a clergyman, probably in reference to the black robes that they wore professionally.

The word seems to have started as a Greek word, *gagate*—a black stone—then passed through Old French and into Old English. Gagate is not a misspelling of agate, by the way.

Another use of the word came from a French term meaning to throw or cast. One of its uses is to describe water spurting from a small orifice. It is also the jet embedded in jet stream, and it accounts for the jet in jet engine.

Another form of jet seems to have come from the Latin *jactare*, to brag or boast, and it was used to describe a strutting, ostentatious walk.

Q.   While driving out to Benzonia this morning I passed the Cherry Growers facility and noticed the stacks of containers used for transporting cherries. I know that they are called "lugs". My question is about the origin of the word lug and its usage as a noun, verb or prefix. For example...*The orchard produced 100 lugs of cherries.* Or, *We had to lug the containers up the hill.* Or, *Our luggage was lost by the airline.* Is there a connection between these three usages? Now I must go tighten the lug nuts on my car!

A.   Interesting question. As it turns out, the lug used to haul cherries and the luggage that we take on trips are connected. They came from an Old Swedish word that meant to move something slowly and heavily, to drag it along. Long before that, the original lug meant to pull a person's hair.

The lug that shows up in lug nut or lug wrench doesn't seem to be directly connected. Instead, it comes from a word that meant a projecting part. Originally, it came from a Scandinavian word that meant the ear flap of a cap, or the ear itself.

In the 1930s, lug also meant a lout, a sponger, a bozo, and a lowlife.

Finally, I can't resist passing along a lug nut story. It appeared in the Kitsap (Washington) Sun on November 10, 2007.

Kitsap Man Hurts Himself Trying to Loosen Lug Nut — With a Shotgun

A 66-year-old man shot himself in both his legs Saturday afternoon while trying to loosen a stubborn lug nut with a 12-gauge shotgun.

Kitsap County sheriff's deputies were called to the residence on the xxxxx block of SE Olympiad Drive at 2:57 p.m. after the shooting was reported to 911 emergency dispatchers, said Deputy Scott Wilson, a sheriff's office spokesman.

"Nobody else was there and he wasn't intoxicated," Wilson said.

South Kitsap Fire and Rescue medics treated the man at the scene. He was taken to Tacoma General Hospital. Wilson said his injuries were "severe but not life-threatening."

Deputies at the scene reported the man blasted "double-ought" buckshot at the wheel from "arm's length," Wilson said.

The deputies described the man's legs as "peppered" from his feet to his mid-abdomen with pellets, pieces of the wheel and other debris. Some injuries went as far up as his chin.

The man had been repairing the Lincoln Continental for two weeks, and had removed all the lug nuts on the right rear wheel except for one.

"He's bound and determined to get that lug nut off," Wilson said, who did not know how long the man had been trying to free the lug nut.

The deputies did not take a statement from the man beyond what they were able to gather while he was being treated by medics.

"I don't think he was in any condition to say anything," Wilson said. "The pain was so severe, and the shock."

180

Next - Topical Index

Punctuation

Word History

Biographical Note

Michael Sheehan taught English classes for 26 years in the City Colleges of Chicago. He is a member of the Society of Midland Authors, the Dictionary Society of North America, American Dialect Society, and Michigan Writers.

This book is a compilation of questions and answers heard on *Words to the Wise,* a weekly radio program (Tuesdays, 9:00 a.m. to 10:00) airing on WTCM, AM 580, Traverse City, Michigan.

Sheehan is a member of the State Advisory Council on Aging (Michigan), the advisory board of the Area Agency on Aging of Northwest Michigan, and of the Bay Area Senior Advocates, a consortium of agencies and services which deal directly with senior citizens in lower northwest Michigan. In addition, he runs a web site for senior citizens which is sponsored by the Traverse Area District Library It is called *The Senior Corner,* and it may be found at http:/ /seniors.tcnet.org

Mike lives in Leelanau County, Michigan, with his artist wife Dona and with Rosa Rugosa, a Neapolitan Mastiff who enjoys a good manuscript from time to time unless she is caught.